A History
of
St. Marie's Cathedral and Parish

Part Three

From the close of the Great War

to becoming a cathedral church

1920 – 1980

Deacon Bill Burleigh

Acknowledgements

In this third part of my history of St. Marie's, I have been able to collect memories from older parishioners and others in their seventies, eighties or nineties. Accounts and anecdotes that I have included stretch back into the 1930s. In addition, souvenirs, orders of service and other ephemeral printed items have been found and provided. All of this, I hope, adds to the clarity of the picture drawn of the parish over the decades described. Through these means I have been able to record the names of parishioners otherwise long forgotten and to keep alive the memory of their contribution to the life and growth of Catholic life as lived through St. Marie's. Among the very many who have provided me with valuable material are the late May Westmoreland, the late Cecil Higgins, the late Ted Cummings; also Mary Hirst, Eileen Maher, Peter Lodge, Bryan Beedham, Brenda Stainrod and Paul Helliwell. I am grateful for all the first hand information I have received.

I want to thank Fr. Chris Pozluszney for his support in my endeavours to produce this book and for the loan of the remaining Sheffield Catholic Monthly parish magazines located at St Marie's. I am also grateful for the considerable support of Bob Rae in processing aging photographs and taking new photographs where needed. I am also grateful for the help of Dr Paul Walker for detailed information on the various changes to the fabric and decoration of St Marie's over the period of this history. I would especially like to thank George Dawn of Mensa Printers for his skillful help in the design and setting of this book. Additionally I am grateful for help received from the Sheffield Local Studies Library and Sheffield Archives, as well as from the diocesan archive of the Diocese of Leeds.

I am particularly grateful for pictures sourced from the Picture Sheffield collection of the Local Studies Library. Additional photographs have been generously provided by Sheffield Newspapers Ltd (pages 31, 51, 55, 72 and 77). Photographs have also been generously provided by the Sisters of Notre Dame (pages 4 and 16), the Little Sisters of the Poor (page 8) and from the estate of the late Vic Hallam (on pages 25 and 26) and from private publications of the Polish community of Sheffield (pages 35, 36 and 37). But most of all, I am grateful for the photographs and mementoes provided from the personal collections of Eileen Maher, Mary Hirst, the family of May Westmoreland, Bryan Beedham, Tony Danaher and Mavis Hamilton. Without all of these contributions it would not have been possible to produce the history in the style I have been able to achieve.

Design: George Dawn

Proof-reading: Liz Caban

Published by: St. Marie's Cathedral Books

Copyright © Bill Burleigh 2018

ISBN 978-0-9575781-5-9

Printed by: Mensa Printers, 111 Arundel Lane, Sheffield S1 4RF

Cover photograph: St. Marie's and surrounding area in the 1930s.

Contents

Foreword

I am pleased that Deacon Bill Burleigh has now produced Part III of his *History of St. Marie's Cathedral and Parish*. This third part covers the years from 1920 until 1980 and the establishment of the Diocese of Hallam with St. Marie's as its cathedral.

Because much of this time period is within living memory, Deacon Bill has been able to draw on direct experience of Catholic life in the city and in the parish as far back as the 1930s. Many of these personal contributions by the elderly enliven the text and give insights not otherwise obtainable. It is remarkable how many names of parishioners over several generations appear in the unfolding narrative. Through interviews, long forgotten souvenirs held by parishioners and plain research, Bill has been able to present material in such a way as to capture something of the mood and feel of the parish and Catholic life in Sheffield at different stages of the 60 years covered.

I found whilst reading this book that I became drawn to read on, gaining a greater appreciation of the depth of faith, generosity and support for parish and people lived by the generations preceeding ours. Firm foundations were laid for us and we benefit even now from so much hard and devoted work freely given in building up not only the parish of St. Marie's but also its many daughter parishes.

In this third part of his history, Deacon Bill completes the long journey of Catholics in Sheffield from the suppression of Catholicism in 1549, through the persecutions, trials and real hardships in Tudor, Stuart and Georgian times, into the 19th century of recovery and through 130 years of lively and expanding parish life at St. Marie's. I am grateful for the long hours it must have taken to produce this fascinating and inspiring narrative.

+ Ralph Heskett CssR

Bishop of Hallam

The former High Altar built in 1921.
This altar stands on the position of the original 1850 High Altar.
The Pugin designed angel reredos for that altar is visible to either side and behind this replacement altar

Chapter I
The Memorial Altar of 1921

On Sunday July 1st 1921 a new High Altar of St. Marie's was solemnly dedicated within High Mass celebrated by Bishop William Keatinge, Bishop to the British Forces. The altar had been commissioned by Canon Oswald Dolan, the Parish Priest of St. Marie's, who had served as an army chaplain throughout the Great War. The new altar was to be a war memorial commemorating the 68 men of the parish who had given their lives in that conflict.[1]

The idea of building a replacement High Altar as a war memorial *"was the spontaneous wish of the people, and with the wish went the determination that it should be the best possible* [in design and execution] *in consonance with the dignity of the church".*[2]

Such an idea and decision shows exceptional appreciation of all that those who went to war had sacrificed. The High Altar of any church, in Catholic understanding of the Eucharist, is the principal place of sacrifice. At the High Altar the sacrifice of Christ is made present in the consecration of bread and wine. It is the focal point of everyone assembled. To choose to replace the 1850 consecrated and perfectly serviceable altar was a serious undertaking that clearly had huge meaning both for Canon Dolan and for the parishioners.

Despite post-war austerity and deepened poverty for many, parishioners rallied and raised the necessary funds. A year before, in the Summer of 1920, *The Tablet* reported that the Duchess of Norfolk had lent her garden at The Farm, Granville Road, for a garden party to raise funds for the memorial altar. At this gathering, the Lord Mayor had *"commended the desire of the congregation to raise a memorial that should be both lasting and beautiful".* A year later, the new altar was complete.

The High Mass of dedication[3] was reported the next day in *Sheffield Daily Telegraph*:

"Prior to the service the procession of the clergy from the Sacristy to the church[4] *attracted considerable public attention, many people kneeling to receive the bishop's blessing. A guard of honour was formed by the St. Marie's Boy Scouts".*

Inside the church, Bishop Keatinge officiated in the presence of the Bishop of Leeds, Dr. Joseph Cowgill[5]. Canon Dolan and Fr. Collingwood[6] flanked Bishop Cowgill. A young curate of St. Marie's, Fr. Maloney, was deacon and Fr. O'Shea of St. Ann's Deepcar was sub-deacon. A choir of *"about forty"* priests[7] sang parts of the Mass in Gregorian chant.

The Provincial of the English Dominicans and renowned writer, Fr. Bede Jarrett, preached[8]. His sermon resonates in its challenge even almost 100 years later. Speaking of the Great War so recently ended he asked the congregation, *"To what purpose is this waste?"*

He went on to denounce

"...those great prophets of ours" ...[who now proclaim] *that if we had only devoted our energies to the homes of the poor or to the education of our children...[then] our hearts would not be so weary or so broken...But, were these better objects than justice, liberty and truth?"* Even *better homes",* he asked, *"were they more desirable than justice, liberty and truth?"*

Then came the challenge:

"How is the nation shaping?...You are the nation....It is in your own lives that the question must be answered... Judge your own heart. What have you each learned,

---

1   Sheffield Daily Telegraph of June 22nd reported the forthcoming dedication of the new altar, citing that it also commemorated the more than "700 of the youth of the parish" who left home and family to join the armed forces.
2   Sheffield Daily Telegraph June 22nd 1921.
3   Details from The Tablet July 4th 1921.
4   Clearly an outdoor procession along Norfolk Row.
5   Prior to 1966, Mass was celebrated by only one priest or bishop. It was customary, when a visiting bishop was celebrating the Mass, for the local bishop to be present, attending the Mass from a place of honour on the sanctuary.
6   A leading Jesuit priest of the time who lived close to Sheffield, at Mount St. Mary's, Spinkhill.
7   *Sheffield Daily Telegraph* 2nd July 1921. But more likely to be laymen dressed in cassocks and surplices.
8   The sermon was reported in Sheffield Daily Telegraph.

*individually, out of the sacrifice of these men's lives?...
These men died for a great vision…What are you going
to do with the thing they died for?...Watch yourself,
watch your public life, watch your politics, whatever side
you are on…Let the memory of these men who died…
be a perpetual challenge to the living to answer these
questions"* [9].

Fr Thomas Moloney

*Bishop Joseph Cowgill
Bishop of Leeds, 1911 - 1936*

Appendix One gives more detail about the Memorial
Altar, its design and how much, if anything, remains of
the original altar designed by A.W.Pugin.

Six days earlier on Monday June 27th, Bishop Cowgill had
come to St. Marie's to consecrate the new altar. *Sheffield
Daily Telegraph* reported the event the following day.
*"Yesterday, in the presence of a large congregation, the
ceremony of consecrating the new High Altar, which had
been erected by the parishioners of St Marie's…to the
memory of the men of the parish who fell in the war…".*

Within the altar were placed the relics of apostles
(previously deposited in the original High Altar by
Bishop Briggs in September 1850) and relics of St.
Vincent (deacon) and St. Tranquilinus[10]. Canon Dolan
and his curate Fr. Maloney assisted, together with seven
other priests, three of whom were Marists[11].

9   There are signs in this sermon there was a backlash to the war and evidence of public dissent, perhaps related to the fatigue
     with war and suffering felt both in Germany and in Britain.
10   Information from Sheffield Archive ref 1995/78. All these relics are now within the new 2013 High Altar at St. Marie's.
11   Frs. Kielty, Russell and Wilson.

Chapter II
The Parish Settles – The 1920s and 1930s

A Catholic Hospital in the Parish

In the afternoon of the same day as the dedication of the War Memorial High Altar at St. Marie's, Bishop Cowgill formally opened the new Catholic hospital facility at Claremont Place, off Glossop Road[12]. Assisting him were the clergy from the morning dedication Mass including Bishop Keatinge, Canon Dolan, Fr. Bede Jarrett OP and Fr. Collingwood SJ. To greet them were the community of Sisters of Mercy, who were to run the new facility, together with their Mother Superior, Sister Agnes.

Sheffield Daily Telegraph reported[13] that the new *"nursing home"* was *"admirably equipped"*. It would be able to take both medical and surgical cases because of the *"well-equipped operating theatre"*. The wards, it wrote, had a *"light and airy appearance"*. The home was, in general, *"charmingly situated"* giving a *"delightful prospect over the Derbyshire hills"*. The *"immediate prospect"* was *"over pleasant lawns and tastefully laid out gardens"*.

Perhaps more importantly, the newspaper report refers to the *"need that the Catholic community of Sheffield and district has felt acutely for some time past"* to have its own medical facility. The need for Catholic schools had long been provided and a priority. The needs of Catholic elderly were being met by the Little Sisters of the Poor beginning in Burngreave and then moving on to the purpose built St. Elizabeth's home at Heeley. Now the new Claremont "nursing home" would meet the need for a Catholic hospital.

The representatives of the Catholic laity at the official opening included some of the medical practitioners. The invited laity reported in the newspaper were Dr and Mrs King, Dr and Mrs Mylan, Dr Wiseman, Dr and Mrs Brookman, Mrs Walter Walsh, Mrs Benson, Mrs Wake, Mr and Mrs Durnan, Mr and Mrs T McDonald, Sydney Beech, Mr and Mrs T Carter, Mrs Yates, Mrs Pardon, Mrs McGrath, Mrs Young, Mrs King with Miss Estelle King, Mrs Neal, Mrs Bowen, Mrs Storer and Mrs A Nicholson.

St Marie's during the 1920s

12 On part of the site now occupied by the Hallamshire Hospital. The Catholic hospital moved to Sandygate Road, Crosspool, in 1953. In 1996 the hospital passed from the Sisters of Mercy to a Hospital Management Trust.

13 *Sheffield Daily Telegraph* 2nd July 1921.

A New Convent

By 1919 living space for the Sisters of Notre Dame at Cavendish Street had become very limited. Even with the 1891 extensions to the 1861 building, the growing needs of the school on the same site meant that there was a need for an additional site.

Oakbrook, on Fulwood Road, had been the home of the industrialist Mark Firth until it became a convalescent home for soldiers during World War 1. In 1919 the Notre Dame Sisters bought the property and developed it as a convent, freeing up space at Cavendish Road for the expanding needs of the school.

The New Convent, Oakbrook, 1919

The Cavendish Street convent and school shortly before 1919

The original chapel at Oakbrook converted from a living room.
Notice the fireplace, mantlepiece mirror, wall paper and ceiling mouldings

Canon Dolan's Silver Jubilee

January 1924 saw the delayed silver jubilee celebrations of the arrival of Canon Dolan at St. Marie's. Celebrations were held in the Parish Hall in Townhead Street. The cause of the delay was Canon Dolan's decision that a planned fund raising bazaar for the new De La Salle School should go ahead, rather than a celebration in his honour. But earlier, on the jubilee date itself, the *Sheffield Independent* had written of the Canon as *"an ardent educationalist"* who *"since he was first elected to the school board in 1900* [had] *done much painstaking work in that connection, his wide knowledge and lengthy experience having made him a great asset to the educational authorities of the city... A man of keen judgement and wide sympathies"*[14].

The delayed celebrations were presided over by Fr. James Bradley, a newly arrived curate at St. Marie's. Fr. Hayes, the former and long-suffering curate through the war years was there too. Also present were the Brothers who would run the De La Salle College, the local MP, J.F. Hope, Alderman W. Fenton (Deputy Lord Major) and the vicar of Ecclesall Parish church, Canon Thomas Houghton.

As anniversary gifts from the parish, Canon Dolan was presented with a cope, embroidered by the nuns of Kirkedge, an illuminated address, a cheque for £240 and a portrait in oils.

14   *Sheffield Independent* 15th September 1923.
15   *Our Fathers in Faith* p.128.
16   *The Tablet* October 1923.

After the celebration the canon went on pilgrimage to the Holy Land[15].

Parish Guilds, Sodalities and Associations

Also present at Canon Dolan's jubilee celebrations were several key parishioners who included Tom Darnan, E.G. Dignam, F.G. Morduant, F.W. Boland, Miss Dolan, Mrs Carter (vice president of the Catholic Women's League)

*The old parish hall in Townhead Street
(next to the Sheffield Playhouse)*

and representatives from every Catholic organisation in the city.

And it was the blossoming of many Catholic groups, guilds, sodalities and associations for lay people of every age that was to be a feature of the coming decade. The Catholic Young Men's Association and the Society of St. Vincent de Paul had long been active and important, with large numbers attending meetings and events. In 1921, the bequest of John Molloy, a parishioner of Springvale Road, shows the prominence of Catholic action for those in need providing, as it does, £100 for poor children of Sheffield irrespective of creed, £1000 for the elderly of St. Vincent's parish, £100 each for St. Joseph's Home run by the Daughters of Charity at Walkley and for the SVP groups of the five Sheffield parishes. £200 was given to Canon Dolan for Masses.

That same year in Sheffield, the national executive of the Catholic Confederation of England and Wales met at St. Marie's Parish Hall with Edward Eyre presiding. Speeches addressed Catholic interests including the Trade Union and Co-operative Movements and the Catholic Press and News Association. Again, a vibrant social and political concern is evident.

In 1922 a Sheffield fraternity of Catenians began at St. Marie's and was represented, the following year, at a meeting of Yorkshire Catenians at Leeds where more than 100 attended[16].

In 1924 the Knights of St. Columba were established in the parish with the expressed aims of providing a scholarship place for the De La Salle college, entertaining poor children and raising funds for the school for boys. The first officers were: T. Hickey (Grand Knight), Reed Hague (deputy Grand Knight), J. Pashley (recorder), J. Shepherd (financial secretary), J. Lodge (chancellor), F. Naish (advocate) and Fr. J. Moloney (chaplain).

Notwithstanding these details from an article in *The Tablet*, a former parishioner, Mrs May Westmoreland (nee Gay), born in 1920, recalls[17] that it was her father who had founded the Knights and that it soon attracted over 100 members and was divided into two confraternities. She recalls a Fr. Maundsley as chaplain, rather than Fr. Maloney[18]. Among her earliest memories is attending a KSC meeting and trips out, funded by the Knights. Each year, she recalls, there was a charabanc[19] trip to the seaside at Skegness involving seven or eight coaches and 30 to 40 mothers with children. A photo taken of her at one of these trips[20] was donated for this book.

Mrs Westmoreland also recalls the yearly Catholic Ball at Sheffield City Hall, again organised through the Knights of St Columba and a sell-out event right up until World War II. And then there were the amateur dramatic shows and parties for various occasions that took place at the Parish Hall in Townhead Street. In the Summer there were trips and opportunities for children to join in the pilgrimages to Roche Abbey, Padley and even Walsingham and trips, too, to watch the parish Knight's cricket team as far afield as Edwinstowe.

Major annual events for both Catholics and townspeople in general were the Whit Monday Walks. Catholics from both St. Marie's and surrounding parishes gathered at each of the parish schools in their best clothes and carrying picnic lunches. Banners from different parish sodalities and societies would be unfurled and the walk would set off. The children would lead the procession, walking in file, overseen by their class teachers. In their heyday, these processions included brass or pipe and drum bands and with tableaux on decorated drays pulled by well-brushed horses in polished harnesses loaned, free of charge, by local businesses. Each parish would take a different route from their school to the grounds of The Farm, the Duke of Norfolk's Sheffield home. Here there would be organized games, stalls and entertainments leading up to parish picnics. The day was enjoyed by all.

A seaside studio photograph during the 1927 parish UCM Skegness trip with May Gay, Winnie Parkin and Frs Mosley (Maundsley) and "Fr Mac"

The Farm

The Catholic Whit Walks were quite distinct from Sheffield's general public Whit Walks that also took place each year and ended with singing and musical gatherings in Norfolk Park. Though once a part of the grounds of the Duke's residence, the green area named as Norfolk Park was donated to the city by the Duke in 1911. The more ornamental gardens and the lake, closer to The Farm, remained in Catholic ownership with the Catholics' own Whit Monday festivities taking place there right through into the 1950s. They contiued even after the time when the house was given over to offices from the London

17   Interviewed in 2013
18   Fr. Maloney was appointed as a curate to the parish in 1927
19   The early name for single decked motor coaches
20   Possibly 1930

and North Eastern Railway Company. Eileen Maher remembers, as a child, enjoying the excitement and fun of St. Marie's Whit Walk and playing with other children at this valued annual event. An archive plan of the grounds gives an idea of the grandeur of these gardens which would have been very impressive, especially to the many parishioners who, over the decades, enjoyed the freedom of these grounds which were often in such stark contrast to their own living conditions at home.

The burgeoning charitable and social actions of St.Marie's in the 1920s were always under-pinned by the spiritual life of the parish. One long-established feature of this was the annual pilgrimage to Padley, near Grindleford in Derbyshire. In July 1921, *The Tablet* reported that Canon Dolan attended the pilgrimage with both of his curates and, no doubt, many parishioners too. The train ride from Sheffield would not have been difficult.

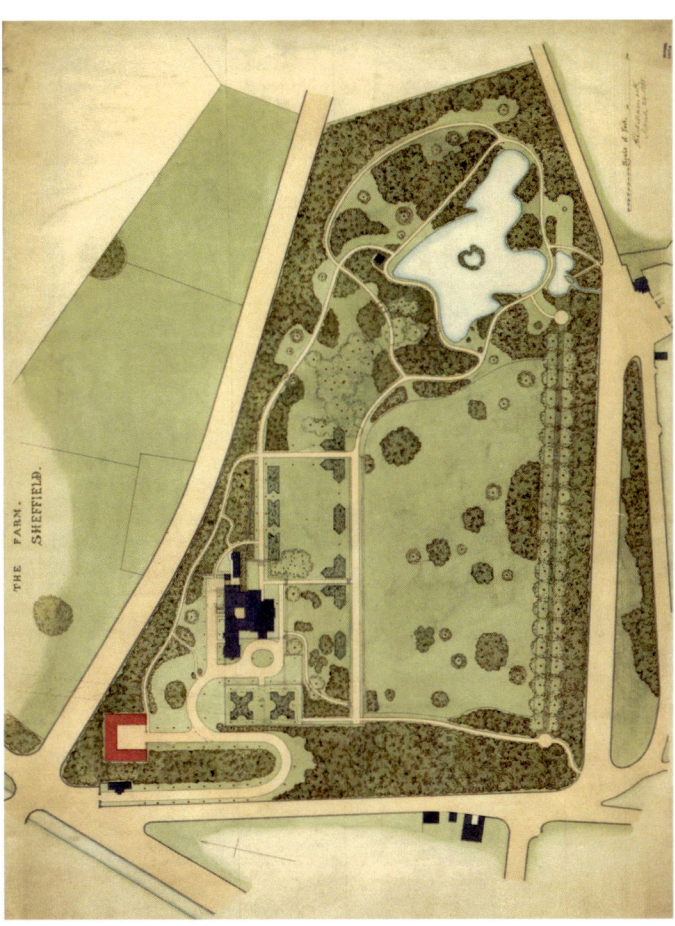

A plan of the grounds of The Farm

Padley Chapel

Mrs Westmoreland remembers, as a teenager in the 1930s, being among the first to join a branch of the Young Christian Workers, started locally by a Fr. Clancy. This international movement enabled young Catholics to become aware of, consider and be involved in social action. Founded in Belgium by a Father (later Cardinal) Cardijn, this movement greatly increased awareness of social injustices, leading to local, supportive action. The principle behind meetings was to reflect on issues and discern what was an appropriate response for the group[21]. Other members of the St. Marie's group were Bernard Sweeney, who also led the SVP, Frank Murphy, who later joined the De La Salle Congregation of Brothers and Nora Connelly.

At the time, the Padley Chapel was in private hands and used as a barn. That year, the Mass for the pilgrims was "said" at St.Michael's in Hathersage, presided over by Fr. Filmer, the national Master of the Guild of Our Lady of Ransom[22]. Banners added to the spectacle as the long procession walked by road from Hathersage to Grindleford and Padley. Sitting on the grass by the chapel, pilgrims heard a sermon from Fr. Daniel Hughes S.J., of Mount St. Mary's College, Spinkhill, who spoke of the 481 people from all parts of the country who, in penal times, were martyrs, in the truest sense of the word. Many more had languished and died for their faith in prisons. In keeping with a local custom that had built up, the pilgrims, the report records, kissed the walls of the chapel before leaving for home.

21   Cardijn's maxim for discernment followed the pattern See, Judge, Act, still a well-used formula in theological reflection.
22   A charitable body to support Anglican converts to Catholicism and a campaign of prayer for the conversion of England back to the Catholic Faith.

St Elizabeth's home for the elderly (above) with residents photographed by the front entrance before 1920 (below)

The foundation stone of St Elizabeth's preserved in a wall among the new houses of St Elizabeth's Close

In 1929, for the centenary of the Catholic Emancipation Act, a small group of male parishioners travelled in Canon Dolan's old Fiat car to the Albert Hall in London to join 7,000 men from across the country and hear Cardinal Bourne as the main speaker[23]. Similarly for men only, eighty parishioners travelled to the 1932 Dublin Eucharistic Conference where an estimated one million men attended the final Pontifical High Mass celebrated in Phoenix Park[24].

An important memory of Catholic life in Sheffield between the two world wars was the constant presence of appeals and the need for fund-raising. Not only did new parishes need support in buildings, but there were the schools, various Catholic buildings and various charitable activities of the lay guilds and societies. During these years, a whole network of Catholic-run support for Catholics of all ages developed. Mrs Westmoreland particularly remembers collecting for the Little Sisters of the Poor and their home for the elderly, St. Elizabeth's, at Heeley and for the support needed in getting new parishes established.

St. Elizabeth's Home stood at the foot of Heeley Bank Road and had beds to accommodate more than 100 elderly Catholics. Originally established in Duchess Road in a small villa obtained through the St Marie's Conference of the Society of St. Vincent de Paul and

Canon Walshaw, the Home needed bigger premises by 1890. With the help of the Duke of Norfolk, who laid the foundation stone, new premises for 75 residents were built between Farm Road and Queen's Road, on the edge of the grounds around the Duke's Sheffield home. A further expansion took place in 1907 after new premises were built in Heeley Bank Road[25].

This building was substantial, described from memory as of red-brick, 4/5 storeys high and with a lift inside. The chapel was a separate building adjoining the back of the main blocks and there were outbuildings for laundry and other maintenance functions. The gardens were closed except for an annual Summer fete. There were statues in the gardens and in alcoves along the outer wall. St. Elizabeth's continued to care for the elderly until 1985 when the building was demolished, it was recalled, with some difficulty because of how well it had been built[26]. Parts of the perimeter wall and the gatehouse can still be seen and the foundation stone is preserved in a wall within the new housing of St. Elizabeth's Close, recalling the Home and the Little Sisters of the Poor.

As far back as 1905 Canon Dolan had established a monthly parish magazine which was produced through into the 1950s. Sadly, few copies are still extant. The earliest copies found date from 1935 and the range of parish clubs, guilds, societies and confraternities can be seen.

The parish magazines give information on more than 12 parish groups meeting each month.

For girls and young adult Catholics there were several groups. The Children of Mary was a devotional group for older girls and young women. They met on the first Sunday of each month in the Parish Room under the care of one of the Notre Dame sisters. The Guild of St. Agnes met every Sunday under the sister in charge of the Girls' School. Once a month, each society came together at a designated Sunday Mass to receive Holy Communion together.

For boys there was the St. Marie's Scout troop under the leadership of Scoutmaster Mr A. Wood. The scouts met in the parish hall in Townhead St. on Thursday evenings, whilst the Wolf Cubs met there on Wednesdays. The Church Parade for both troops was on the fourth Sunday of each month. There was also the Guild of St. Stephen for the altar servers. For the more musically inclined, there was the Boys' Choir whose members were rewarded each Christmas for their singing at Mass and other services during the year. They were treated to a turkey and plum pudding Christmas dinner and a trip to

23   See Fr. John Ryan's *St. Marie's Cathedral History and Guide*, (1989).
24   Also in Ryan (1989) but the source parish magazines are no longer traceable.
25   Evinson, Denis: *The Lord's House* (1991, Sheffield Academic Press).
26   A blogger on SheffieldForum.co.uk/showthread.php.145806.

the pantomime. At Easter the choirmaster would give them an Easter Egg each.

For young women and mothers there was the Guild of St. Ann, who met in the Parish Room on Monday afternoons under the care of a Sister of Charity. For women more generally the parish hosted the Sheffield Branch of the Catholic Women's League whose chairperson in 1935 was Mrs. Pardon of Westbourne Road, and later Mrs C. Simpson[27]. By 1937, a branch of the Legion of Mary also had been formed at St. Marie's to be a spiritual army against the world and its evil powers[28]. At the annual *Acies* (latin for a battle formation) ceremony, each Legionary approached the Lady altar, renewing their dedication by pledging "I am all thine, my Queen, my Mother and all I have is thine" whilst holding the local branch's flag. In 1938 it was the turn of St. Mary's parish at Mortomley to host the Acies and fifteen Legionaries travelled there from St. Marie's for the ceremony.

Emblems of the Legion of Mary

For men there was the long-established Society of St. Vincent de Paul who met in the Parish Room on Mondays, and the Catholic Club under its president Charles Sweeney[29]. Again, all these societies, both those for men and those for women, met together at one Mass each month to receive Holy Communion as a group. In addition, of course, there was the Men's Choir who sat in the stalls in the sanctuary at High Mass to sing both plainchant and other music.

With more general membership there was the Arch-confraternity of the Rosary who met monthly on a Sunday under the care of Fr. Maudsley, one of the curates. The Arch-confraternity of the Blessed Sacrament met on the fourth Sunday of each month for an hour of adoration. The parish ran a Catholic library from which books could be borrowed for one penny each. The Choral Society held rehearsals every Monday evening at St. Vincent's. In 1935 its president was P. Fitzsimmons, its spiritual director was the curate Fr. O'Leary and its chairman was Mr C. Sweeney.

For all, the centre of parish life was, of course, the Mass which was celebrated on Sundays at 7am, 8am, 9.45am (children's Mass) and 11am. Later in the day there was a Children's Service with Benediction at 3pm and, later, Vespers, Sermon and Benediction at 6.30pm. On weekdays, besides two daily morning Masses , there was Rosary, a talk and Benediction each Wednesday evening and Rosary with a litany each Saturday evening. Confessions were heard before every Mass, on the Thursday evening before each first Friday of the month and, weekly, on Saturdays from 4.30 – 6pm and 7 -9pm.

In all, the parish was religiously very active.

Norfolk Row between the Wars

27   In an interview in 2014, Mary Hirst remembered her mother (Mrs Laura Hirst) being active in and a chairperson of CWL. She recalled the active involvement of a Mrs McGrath who had lost her husband in the Great War and had two surviving children, having lost a baby boy. Despite her difficulties, she was a willing helper with even the most basic or necessary of tasks.

28   Constitution of the Legion cited in Sheffield Catholic Monthly, April 1938.

29   This group always provided a Christmas Treat for the children of the parish. In 1935, 86 sat down to tea which was followed by a concert.

Chapter III
Fund Raising and Building – So Much and So Often

The city in the 1930s, showing the many factory chimneys

Sheffield between the Wars

As the munitions factories, which had expanded so hugely during World War One, were reduced down to peace-time requirements, unemployment in Sheffield began to rise sharply. At the same time, large numbers of men had returned to the labour force from military service. The economic depression of the 1920s soon followed. Severe unemployment with its resulting poverty lasted, in Sheffield, throughout the 1920s and 1930s.

One of the effects of on-going poverty and the desperation it brings to families was the rise of illegal gambling across Sheffield. A game of chance, known as "pitch and toss" was played on street corners[30], outside factory gates on pay days and, with largest numbers of people taking part, at Sky Edge, an open space off City Road[31]. This illegal and exploitative business was only controlled through the eventual suppression of Sheffield's powerful and violent gangs in the late 1920s.

Some relief from the poor housing, unhealthy living conditions and the smog of life in the city began in Sheffield with the building of the first local authority housing estates. The Manor Estate was the first of these, built on land purchased from the Catholic Duke of Norfolk in 1919. A total of 3,754 houses were planned, and construction began in 1923. There was serious criticism of the plans, especially the lack of public buildings such as schools and churches. In 1926 there were over 3,000 school-aged children on the Manor Estate and school places for only 232 in the wooden huts that were provided as schools. It was one of these huts that Canon Dolan rented as a church before going on to organise the building of St. Theresa's school.

Whilst slum clearances began in the early 1920s to make space for the proposed Woburn Estate, the anti-Labour coalition responsible for its construction failed to provide either hot water or electricity as a standard. Tenants were to pay two shillings a week to have these extras.

---

30   More than one old person visited by me (the author) within my ministry over the past fifteen years has spoken of the desperation of fathers gambling the family's tiny income in the hopes of winning enough to cover current needs and to pay off some debts. The children knew what was going on with the huddles of men gathered around a 'toller' (the man linked to the gangs who set the toll or charge that had to be paid by the winner from their winnings). There was always a look-out person watching for any policeman that might discover them.

31   It is recorded that upwards of 200 men at a time would gather at Sky Edge, taking part in games of pitch and toss, around large numbers of gang-linked tollers and their look-outs (crows).

It was this sort of parsimony, as well as poor building workmanship by private contractors, that aided the election of a long lasting Labour city council which used its own work force to build better houses. New housing was accelerated most notably through the 1930s. Between 1923 and 1939, Sheffield built 28,000 council houses, with 16,000 on the Manor alone, 5,362 on the Parson Cross Estate, 4,472 at Shiregreen, and 4,472 at Arbourthorne. All these estates would have churches and schools built for their Catholic populations, each in a parish that was a daughter or grand-daughter parish of St. Marie's.

But Sheffield's centre remained far from clean or healthy. Though Sheffield's slum clearance and replacement housing programme in the 1930s was the largest in the country, extreme poverty and foul living conditions were still commonplace. Visiting Sheffield in 1936 to research for his book, *The Road to Wigan Pier*, George Orwell described Sheffield as "*the ugliest town in the Old World*". In his diary for 3rd March that year, noted whilst in Sheffield, he writes,

"*On the one hand the new housing schemes in Sheffield are immensely superior, and on the other hand the Sheffield slums are more squalid than anything London can show...I have travelled almost the whole city. It seems to me, by daylight, one of the most appalling places I have ever seen. In whichever direction...monstrous chimneys...You can smell the sulphur in the air all the while...I counted factory chimneys and I could see there were thirty three...[the] mean little houses [were] blackened by smoke*".

But Orwell acknowledges both that "*The town is being torn down and rebuilt at an immense speed*" and that there is a "*superiority*" and a dignity in the Sheffield working class families at home who live "*without the pretensions*" and ensuing pressures "*that beset more middle class families*". Orwell would have been unusually impressed by the Catholic families on the Manor with their communal efforts to provide time, energy and money to build a school and then a church amidst what he described as an "*estate... at the very summit of a hill, on horrible sticky clay soil and swept by icy winds*". Sheffield working class people, he saw, could shine through their appalling conditions.

Daughter Parishes

St. Marie's has eight daughter parishes, all but one established between 1850 and 1940. In 1853 the invited arrival of Vincentian priests heralded the founding of St. Vincent's parish. St. Charles parish followed from the founding of a chapel in Salmon Pastures in 1864 and the opening of St. Charles' church in 1868.

The residents of the slum dwellings in Allen Street in 1937

Architectural drawing for the building of St Charles, Attercliffe in 1868

The Interior of St Wilfred's Church in the 1920s

The Exterior of St William's in the 1920s

Then, in 1879, came St. Wilfrid's in Shoreham Street, close to the new St. Marie's boys' school under the De La Salle Brothers.

St. Williams in Ecclesall Road started with the opening of a chapel of ease there in 1905, moving out from the chapel near Paradise Square and becoming a parish in 1935.

The 1856 mission of St. Catherine in Andover Street took time to develop in the poverty of its area, but the new parish of St. Catherine was eventually formed and the new church on Burngreave Road was opened in 1926.

The story of the beginnings of St. Theresa's parish was probably first written down in or around 1955 by Frank Walsh, one of those who first caused that parish to form. In his booklet he recalls the enthusiastic beginnings and the struggles to bring the Mass to the large and new Manor estate, then separated from Sheffield by "*bleak agricultural land*"[32].

As a "*vigorous youthful supporter of St. Marie's football Club*", Frank probably walked the distance from the estate to St. Marie's more than most other Catholics living on the estate, which was at the very edges of the parishes of St. Marie's, St. Charles, St. Wilfrid's at Heeley Bottom and St. Joseph's at Handsworth. Getting to Mass at St. Marie's by 9.45am on a Sunday morning was difficult, even when the tram was running and on time. On one occasion during 1927, Frank recalls, he met up with others on their way to Mass at St. Marie's. Someone said "*What about getting Mass up here*"(on the Manor), to which the reply was "*If you want it, 'we' will have to get it. It's the laity who build churches; priests occupy them*". The following week further thought was given and on the third week, names were taken of those few who travelled down to Mass from the Manor and an impromptu meeting was held at the Commercial Street bus terminus. The parish, he writes, was born there.

An approach was made to Canon Dolan to supply a priest for Mass on the Manor. "*Go and find Catholics up there and then come and tell me the number*", came the reply. And the task of finding Catholics, their numbers, ages of children and school needs began by laboriously visiting house by house as one Catholic family identified another to be visited, until the network of a parish began to form. This census revealed about 120 Catholics[33]. Canon Dolan agreed to provide Mass on the estate and rented a school hut there from the Local Authority for use as a Mass centre on Saturday evenings.

Frank Walsh recalls that Canon Dolan brought with him the altar stone, chalice and vestments he had used as a chaplain in France. Between each Saturday evening Mass and the next, the heavy collapsible table (used as the altar) was stored upright in the bathroom of a local Catholic family and the vestments and other items tidied away into a dressing table drawer. On Saturdays, families from all over the estate made their way to the rented school hut. It took a while for the neighbours to

32   Frank Walsh *History of St. Theresa's,* transcribed from the original manuscript by Betty Sherwood.
33   Brenda Stainrod remembers, as a child, living at 11 Desmond Crescent. In the same street there were Catholic families at numbers 6 (the Cottons), 10 (the Stringers), 22 (the Monagans) and, around the corner in Beaumont Road, the Kellys and the Shearins.

work out why so many people were going to school on Saturday evenings.

At Eastertide children would receive First Holy Communion even though there was no Catholic school for them to attend. Frank's account clearly shows pride in the fact that it was lay people on the estate who prepared children for the Sacraments. In Summer, with up to 120

ST. THERESA'S NEW SCHOOL,
MANOR ESTATE.

The Cost, £12,000.   Wanted, £8,000.

Could You Spare a Poor Dog a Bone?
DON'T SAY
The Cupboard is Bare.
LOOK AGAIN. I THINK
THE LITTLE FLOWER
Has put something there for me. We are in desperate need of Help and grateful for any donation however small.

We Offer Holy Mass every week for Benefactors.

CANON DOLAN,
ST. MARIES',
SHEFFIELD.

SIR W. C. LENG & CO. (SHEFFIELD TELEGRAPH), LTD., ALDINE COURT.

A fundraising poster for a new school on the Manor

people packed into the hut *"the atmosphere could be unbearable"*. A door was opened behind the altar and *"there was an unobstructed view over the hills from Ringinglow to Kirkedge"*. All through the year meetings were held in a pub, planning *"unstintingly, whist drives, dances, concerts and socials"*.

Time passed, but two years later, in 1929, land was purchased and a foundation stone for a school was laid by Bishop Cowgill. St. Marie's continued to be the

mother church, supplying a priest for Mass in the school hall. The day eventually came when a small band from the Manor borrowed the open-topped tourer car from St. Marie's and enthusiastically set off to Leeds to buy a monstrance, sanctuary lamp and stations of the cross – the fruits of more fund-raising. *"The wind and the rain froze the blood in our veins nearly"* Frank Walsh wrote in his history.

The tabernacle for the altar was made in a Catholic house on the estate by a non-Catholic well-wisher. From this school hall, all the services of a parish developed. In 1934 the parish was formally founded and a church built and opened in 1938.

No sooner was St. Teresa's parish founded and efforts in fund-raising for its church at their height, than a further new parish was needed, this time on the Wybourn Estate, where a school was planned as a first step[34]. Canon Dolan wrote in St. Marie's parish magazine in Autumn 1935,

"The new school at Wybourn will test the financial resources of this parish to the utmost limit…I think we can take on this burden…I want parishioners to be aware of the fact that there will be financial difficulties ahead. I must have the co-operation of every parishioner. Those who refuse to support this appeal will be turning a deaf ear to the cries of little children. Further, when I say you must help, I mean that there must be self-sacrifice of such a sort that it hurts".

Canon Dolan was a plain speaking man. Entries in the St. Marie's parish magazine confirm a range of fund-raising ventures towards the costs of the school at Wybourn. Though St. Marie's funded a rented school chapel from 1935, the foundation stone of a dedicated replacement was laid on Easter Sunday 1939. The official opening of a chapel dedicated to Our Lady, Queen of Heaven and St. Oswald took place in 1940, but it would take until 1955 before the present church for could be built on the Wybourn estate[35].

The last of the daughter parishes of St. Marie's was at Crosspool. A few older people still recall the long walk to St. Marie's from Fulwood, Crosspool or, even, Lodge Moor Hospital. It was not until 1954 that a chapel of ease became available in a redundant school room and former library. Supplied from St. Marie's until 1968, this hall went on to serve as the church of the new daughter parish of St. Francis[36].

---

34   As the estate grew, Mass was initially celebrated on Sundays in the Catholic chapel of City Road Cemetery. Then a classroom in a new council school on the estate was used. Then, when it was built, the parish met for Mass in the school chapel of what grew to be St. Oswald's school.

35   The parish was renamed simply as St. Oswald's in 1985 but is now known again by its original dedication.

36   For more than 30 years until land was donated by Miss Marion Young of The Croft, on which the present church was built in 1989.

Sheffield's Catholic Schools in the 1920s and 1930s

In 1929 Cardinal Bourne came to Sheffield to open the new St Theresa's school on the Manor, built for 400 children. He was met at the station by Canon Dolan and representatives of some of the societies of St Marie's parish. Next day (9th March) he celebrated High Mass at St. Marie's at which he spoke of his concern that current government proposals requiring more schools would (as before in 1902) leave Catholics at an unfair financial disadvantage. The proposals were for nationwide reductions in class sizes, raising the school leaving age to 15 and for new middle age-band "central" schools. All three would create the need for new schools or large numbers of extensions and would greatly increase costs. Catholic schools, Cardinal Bourne argued, would need an equal measure of additional money as any non-denominational Local Authority school. But there was no clarity in policy nor any guarantee that any funding for the additional building for Catholic schools would come from the government. Eventually, the 1936 Education Act introduced "special agreement" schools for the Catholic community which offered up to 75% of additional building costs provided that staff became employees of the Local Education Authority, and not the church or school.

By 1930, children in St. Marie's parish were served by a complete array of Catholic schools. There was the St. Marie's boys' elementary school (St. Edmund's) in Edmund Road run by the De La Salle brothers.

At Sheaf Gardens there was St. Marie's elementary school for girls[37]. When aged 11, some girls passed entry exams for Notre Dame; those who did not pass stayed

St Maries Boys' School in Edmund Road

on at St. Marie's until they reached the leaving age of fourteen.

For older boys there was the De La Salle College[38] at Scott Road, Osgathorpe[39], the school which had been achieved through the sheer determination of Canon Dolan over many years and finally opened in 1924.

For older girls there was the Cavendish Road senior school for girls run by the Notre Dame Sisters. In addition, there was the fee paying school for girls at Burngreave run by the Sisters of Mercy.

Edmund Road De La Salle Brothers
Casimir (Patrick Dooney), Pius (Joseph Long),
Leander (Thomas McGrath) and Matthew (Walter Bolger)

Convent of Mercy, Burngreave Road

37   St. Marie's school was close to where the River Sheaf flowed into a culvert beneath the city centre. Mary Hirst, interviewed in 2013, recalls a day when a child, pulling on her coat in the cloakroom at the end of the day, suddenly screamed. A rat had settled in the sleeve during the day.

38   Opened in 1923.

39   Off Barnsley Road, between Pitsmoor and Firvale.

In the early 1930s, the Notre Dame sisters moved their convent from Cavendish Street to Oakbrook, at Fulwood. In 1935 an extension of the girls' school was opened on that site, providing additional space and school places.

New Oakbrook High School 1935

During the following year, the *Catholic Herald*[40] reported the unveiling of a marble statue of Blessed Julie Billiart[41], the foundress of the Notre Dame congregation. Present as a guest of honour at that unveiling was Mrs. Bernascone, then aged 87. She had been invited there because she had been *"the first pupil of Notre Dame [school] in 1856"*[42].

Mr and Mrs Bernascone were prominent members of St. Marie's congregation and both were major benefactors of Catholic causes across Sheffield. In 1930, John Bernascone, owner of Bernascone and Company (Sheffield and Paris), died aged 80. His will shows[43] both his generosity and the breadth of his support for Catholic social action. He left £500[44] to the Little Sisters of the Poor who ran the home of the elderly at the foot of Heeley Bank Road; £500 for the Notre Dame teaching sisters; £1,000 for the bishop for the development of a parish for the Manor, £100 for the Howard Hill Reformatory, £100 for Sheffield Royal Hospital (aware, no doubt of the Catholic input into that hospital's founding); £100 for Jessop's Hospital for Women and £25 to Canon Dolan for St. Wilfrid's church in Shoreham Street. His widow, Lavinia, went on to fund the entire building costs for the Sacred Heart church at Hillsborough. It was Mrs Bernascone who added to the decoration of St. Marie's with the alabaster statue now known as "the Bernascone angel." which stands in the South transept.

Mrs Lavinia Bernascone

In 1931, too, a last link was lost with the family of Dr. (later Sir) Arnold Knight, whose family, raised in Norfolk Row, went on to make a huge contribution to the life of the Church with three sons ordained as priests and three daughters who became sisters of Notre Dame. Harriet entered the Notre Dame Sisters at Namur in 1864, but sadly died of scarlet fever within a year. Jane followed her into the convent, taking her recently dead sister's religious name of Sister Gertrude. She died in 1898. Dr. Knight's youngest daughter, Lucy, who was baptized in the New Chapel in 1841 and had entered the Notre Dame Sisters as Sister Marie taking the name Marie, died at the age of 90[45].

Within two years, another major figure in the Catholic life of Sheffield died. Philip Wake of Handsworth Grange, magistrate and owner of Wake and Sons (solicitors)[46] had, for many years, been Steward of the Duke of Norfolk for his Sheffield estates, a post held by Catholics since the 18th century.

40   24th July 1936.
41   The statue includes a representation of a school child in 1930s dress said to have been modelled on the daughter of the sculptor, Wilfrid Milburn of York.
42   *The Catholic Herald* 24th July 1936.
43   Reported in *The Tablet* 23 August 1930.
44   Equivalent to £28,650 at 2016 prices.
45   Information from the extensive research by Dr Derek Cullen into the Knight family.
46   By 1933, a company already in business for 130 years.

Chapter IV
Parish Life in the 1930s

Trouble with the Spire and the Bells

By 1930, St. Marie's was 80 years old but little had been yet been needed in terms of repairs to the building's fabric. True, additional windows had been cut, first, in 1873, in the west walls of both the north and the south transept, and then, in 1889, to the clerestory[47]. All these were to add light to the church in its nave and its transepts. Not surprisingly, by the 1930s, repairs and maintenance were becoming necessary. In 1925, a major rebuild was needed to the spire '*owing to subsidence*'[48]. The top third of the spire was taken down and rebuilt. The following year, with the repairs complete, a steel cross and a gilt

A steeplejack decorates the spire of St. Maries for the King's Jubilee in 1935

weathercock were presented by Thomas Firth and Sons, blessed by Canon Dolan and carried up the 57 metres to the top of the spire by Robert Groves, foreman of Messrs Harrison, Steeplejacks.

In 1934 the bells were found to be in need of reconditioning and re-hanging[49]. Alongside this work they were cleaned and tuned. In early 1935, the bells were ready to be peeled again[50]. Later that year, to commemorate King George V's jubilee, the spire was decorated with a crown around the weathercock and a special peel rung out in celebration.

The Death of Canon Dolan

In May 1935 Canon Dolan was in Rome for the canonisation ceremony of St. John Fisher and St. Thomas More. There was a mood of pride and celebration throughout the Catholic Church in England at these canonizations. It had been several centuries since any English person had been declared a saint. Perhaps for Canon Dolan personally, this was particularly special[51]. He had come to St. Marie's in 1898 directly from the parish of English Martyrs in York. This parish had been named after the 54 martyrs, including Bishop John Fisher and Sir Thomas More, beatified by Pope Leo XIII in 1886. Popular devotions to the English martyrs of the Reformation and enthusiasm for the conversion of England back to the Catholic faith were a major theme within Catholic life in England both before and for many decades following these canonizations.

Canon Dolan returned from Rome but, feeling unwell "*within two days of his return to Sheffield, on advice, he was admitted to a nursing home, where he died on Wednesday 29th May 1935 at the age of seventy four*"[52]. The Tablet obituary reports that the canon died shortly before midnight and that "*Canon Robert Dunford of Hillsborough, and other of his fellow clergy, were with him in his last hours*"[53].

47   In 1889 seven new windows had been added, three above the arches on the north side of the nave and four above the south side. The new windows can be identified by the quatrefoil tracery. The original clerestory window all had trefoil tracery.
48   This work was undertaken in 1925 by Charles Flockton of the Sheffield architects' firm Gibbs and Flockton.
49   Mears and Stainbank, the London Whitechapel foundry and makers of the bells, were engaged to undertake this work. The replacement timber frame with steel might also have been to add strength and stability to the tower and the spire above.
50   February edition of *Sheffield Catholic Monthly*.
51   The parish magazine noted that "*He had advocated greater devotion to the English Martyrs for many years*" July 1935.
52   *Our Fathers of Faith* p.129.
53   *The Tablet* 8th June 1935.

The obituary in the *Sheffield Independent* focussed on the quality of Canon Dolan's personal sacrifice and care for his parishioners.

"He was never found wanting, for seldom has a congregation been better served than was St. Marie's by their beloved pastor. For his own personal comfort he was careless, but he was unremitting in his work on behalf of his flock. Money subscribed by his parishioners to give him what they considered some material comfort was spent on schools or on St. Marie's Hall in Townhead Street for the benefit of young people of his parish. Education was to him a matter of real concern, and in this respect he has left his mark upon the Catholic life of the city"[54].

The July edition of St. Marie's parish magazine *The Catholic Monthly* provides a more personal obituary:

"Our dearly beloved Canon is gone from us…We shall all miss him…For one, it will be his capacity for affection, for another, his charming hospitality, for another perhaps, his hearty laughter and jolly humour that could brighten up public and parochial meetings.

"Our dear Canon never laid claim to intellectual profundity or subtlety…His motives were always transparent, and his sincerity obvious. He simply went straight for what he wanted and woe to you if you stood in his way…He was so impersonal an adversary that we still remained his friend – and nobody could bury the hatchet so irretrievably as he could…He was generous but not lavish in his praise, strong and perhaps even a little harsh in his condemnation of irregularities.

"It can truly be said that Canon Dolan was a cultured man…He loved chamber music in his own house … His favourite composer was Beethoven, and after him, perhaps Mendelssohn. In politics he harked back wistfully to the days of Dizzy and Gladstone, when issues were clear, and a fight was really a fight.

"During his long Rectorship of St. Marie's he has invited the ablest of preachers to his church, and it would be difficult to compile a list of all the eminent priests who have responded to his invitations. And was not the Canon's friend, the late Cardinal Bourne, one of the last to do so".

The improvements to St. Marie's under Canon Dolan, leaving aside the War Memorial Altar, are mainly more practical than ornamental. They include the re-flooring of the church, the installation of electric lighting[55], the building of the new presbytery and parish room[56] and the re-hanging of the church bells onto a steel frame.

Canon Dolan's funeral at St. Marie's was very well attended. Among the interests of the canon was his membership of "the Old Chapter". Before 1850, this had been a body of secular priests to assist the three Vicars Apostolic in the governance of the Church in England before dioceses or parishes were legally permitted. After 1850, this equivalent of a cathedral chapter was retained, but simply as an honorary fellowship into which senior or particularly well-regarded secular priests were invited. Canon Dolan was, for many years, a member of this brotherhood and, in later years, had been elected as its president. Many fellow priests travelled to Sheffield for his funeral.

The *Sheffield Independent* reported[57] that *"so great was the procession of cars as the funeral cortege left for Intake Cemetery [now called City Road Cemetery], Sheffield, where the Canon was laid to rest, that traffic was held up for some minutes"*.

Canon Dolan's grave in City Road Cemetery

---

54   *Sheffield Independent 30 May 1935.*
55   St. Marie's was one of the first Sheffield churches to be lit by electricity.
56   Still very much in use today.
57   On 3rd June 1935.

Canon Dolan's Successors

Canon Dolan's successor was quickly appointed. Canon Thomas Bentley took up the post, but, as had happened with the successor to Canon Walshaw 40 years earlier, he was unable to settle and moved on after only a year[58].

Canon Thomas Bentley

His replacement was Fr. James Bradley, born and brought up in the parish and previously serving as a curate before 1920. Once settled, Fr Bradley was honoured as a canon of the diocese and became Canon Bradley, serving at St. Marie's for the next 15 years.

Canon Bradley had, as a boy, attended St. Marie's school on Edmund Road. Having expressed a desire to become a priest, James was sent by Bishop William Gordon to be taught by the monks of Douai Abbey, in France. However the anti-Church government expelled the monks, who then came to England to form an abbey near

Canon James Bradley

Reading. James Bradley continued his studies at Ushaw where he was ordained a priest in 1910. After serving as a chaplain to the forces during the First world War, Fr. Bradley returned to Sheffield as a curate at St. Marie's under Canon Dolan. His appointment as Parish Priest to replace Canon Bentley was, in a sense, a home coming.

Here he served the parish for more than 15 years. His sister, Annie, was his housekeeper throughout these years and is remembered for her strict protection of his privacy and rest.

A Memorial Window

Very swiftly, after the death of Canon Dolan, a parish fund for a fitting memorial to him was started and by 1937 a stained glass window in the Baptistery could be afforded. To the pre-existing window showing the Baptism of Our Lord[59] on the North wall a second and new window was made in the West wall[60] and a memorial to Canon Dolan in stained glass was added. This window[61] shows three saints: Saint Oswald as Canon Dolan's patron saint[62] and the name of the last parish he founded, on Wybourn Estate; St. Therese of Lisieux in remembrance of the

---

58   He was appointed instead to St. Robert's Harrogate.

59   By an unknown artist, dating from the 1920s, and donated to memory of the Golden wedding anniversary of John and Lavinia Bernascone which fell on the feast day of these two apostles.

60   It is unclear whether this was a new window cut into the wall or whether there was an earlier, smaller window which was enlarged to accommodate the memorial window's design.

61   By John Hardman and Co, of Birmingham.

62   The main picture shows the king being blessed (perhaps by St. Paulinus) before the battle, near Hexham, to overcome Cadwalla, a heathen king. Newly baptised, Oswald erected a wooden cross before the battle began and later attributed his victory to this action.

The 1937 memorial window to Canon Dolan

throne, vested in cappa magna and attended by canons in their robes of office"[65]. It was Canon Hudson (Barnsley, Holy Rood), Canon Dunford (Hillsborough, Sacred Heart) and Canon White (Burngreave, St. Catherine's) who assisted the bishop at his throne. Fr. Bradley (St. Marie's) celebrated the Mass. Fr. A. Hewitt assisted as deacon and Fr. Palframan as sub deacon. Also on the sanctuary were Fr. Bennet (Sheffield, St. Vincent's), Fr. Moloney (Ecclesall, St. William's) and Fr. Gallon (Attercliffe, St. Charles). The MCs from the parish were Mr B. Askew and Mr B. Sweeney. Fr. B. Ford (Lane Top, St. Patrick's) preached on the theme of natural light, the light of faith and illumination by God's light.

It is interesting to note from this list of priests how much more developed were the parish structures across Sheffield by 1938 as compared with the parishes existing and represented at the consecration of the new High Altar in 1921.

The fund for Canon Dolan's memorial window closed within a year and the remaining balance paid for the iron railings and gate added to separate the Baptistery from the rest of the church. The speed in collecting the money to pay for the window and the fact that there was enough left over to pay for the embellishment of the baptismal area shows the high esteem in which Canon Dolan was held[66].

From the Parish Magazine 1935 - 1939

Though there are few remaining copies of the monthly parish magazine, a set still exists of all the 1935, 1937 and 1938 editions. The following is a selection of news items from the various years arranged in a single twelve month cycle.

January - The parish branch of the Catholic Games League won trophies for cribbage against other city clubs competing for the Maher Cup. The team won the gold medal for highest break and the gold medal for best aggregate score.

February - On 6th February 1937, Bishop Poskitt celebrated the Sacrament of Confirmation at St. Marie's confirming 303 young children. The names listed in the parish magazine include two, three or even four children from the same family being confirmed together. This indicates that it was several years since the previous visit by the bishop for Confirmation at St. Marie's.

canon's work to build up St. Therese's parish and school on the Manor[63] and St. Jean Baptiste De La Salle, to commemorate Canon Dolan's establishing the Grammar school to be run by De La Salle brothers at Osgathorpe for older Catholic boys[64]. The decorative scroll work includes oak leaves, Canon Dolan having died on Royal Oak Day, May 29th.

On 23rd January 1938, the memorial window was blessed by Bishop H. J. Poskitt of Leeds following High Mass that was celebrated "in the presence of the Bishop at his

---

63   Behind the saint is a depiction of the pilgrimage basilica at Lisieux, on which the dome of the eventual church at the Manor was based. Beneath the saint is an image of Therese at prayer and above, in the tracery, is the Carmelite emblem.

64   Behind the saint is a scene of Rouen, where English boys were sent for Catholic education with St. Jean Baptiste. Beneath, the saint is seen teaching some of these boys. In the tracery above are the arms of the Christian Brothers, founded by St. Jean Baptiste de la Salle.

65   St. Marie's magazine, *Sheffield Catholic Monthly,* February 1938.

66   In the 1988 history of St. Marie's, mention is made of extensive work to the spire similar to that of 1924, but the extant parish magazines of 1935 do not mention this or any debt arising. On the contrary, the focus on the Dolan memorial window and the speedy raising of more than sufficient for this in a brief time raises a doubt as to whether any structural repair work was done on the spire in 1934.

Bishop Henry Poskitt
Bishop of Leeds, 1936- 1950

The result was a draw, though the magazine's detailed commentary suggests that the senior team was hard pressed even to draw against the Juniors.

The annual May Queen procession in church was as fully attended as ever. The May Queen, led by eight girls with baskets of flower petals[69], processed down the central aisle, escorted by two attendants, to crown the statue, Sometimes in the *"Rosary Chapel"* or at the rood screen.

June - The experience of the 1937 Diocesan Pilgrimage to Lourdes[70], with 300 people travelling together, is described in detail. Leaving Sheffield in the early morning, they arrived in London by train at around 2pm and boarded a steamer at Folkestone at 4.20pm. By 8pm they were in Boulogne and enjoying a French dinner before boarding the train for Lourdes and a fitful night's sleep. Breakfast was taken in Poitiers and they eventually reached Lourdes at 4.30pm. Throughout, the report is full of enthusiasm about the pilgrimage.

March - The annual St. Patrick's Night concert at Townhead Street parish hall played to a *"crowded house, as usual"*.

Also the parish club joined together with the Knights of St. Columba, the Guild of St. Stephen and the parish scouts to hold a larger than normal bazaar to raise funds for the Manor school.

April - At the Maundy Thursday Mass, 42 children celebrated their First Holy Communion. The prizes for best and second best essay describing their First Communion Day were won by Patricia Bond and Elsie Westmoreland respectively.

The Eastertide Quarant Ore (Forty Hours) period of adoration in 1938 drew an unexpected visitor. During the night time the church was open, lit up with lights and with worshippers coming and going. At around 3am a policeman entered the church to investigate whether someone had broken in. He was reassured and is reported to have remarked that *"It looked really lovely"*.

May - Whitsun sports took place at The Farm grounds[67]. In the football competition St. Marie's Junior XI (champions and finalists in the Sheffield Schools' Junior Competition in 1938) took on St. Marie's First XI[68].

Boys from St. Maries School
dressed for the 1936 Corpus Christi procession

July - The 1935 list of exam successes in religious education showed 6 distinctions and 12 credit passes for the Higher Religious Certificate and 29 passes at the School level certificate. No students failed their exam.

August - Each year a report was given of the week long camp of the parish scout troop. In 1935 the camp was at Carlton Towers, Goole, with standard scouting camping routines, games and camp fire singing.

67   The Farm in Norfolk Park Road was a home of the Duke of Norfolk who regularly made its grounds available for Catholic use.
68   One of those in this team was Robert Enderby, later the husband of parishioner Mrs Winifred Enderby
       who died in November 2014.
69   Mary Hirst was one of these strewer of petals in the 1937 procession.
       Mary has provided memories for this book in an interview at her home in 2014.
70   This was the 7th annual Lourdes pilgrimage of the diocese

August 1937 saw the wedding of Gerard Young of Richmond Park[71] to Miss Diana Murray, formerly of Sheffield but latterly of Manor Cottage, Worksop. Bishop Poskitt officiated, assisted by Monsignor Marshall, a cousin of the groom. The deacon and sub deacon were Benedictine friends from Ampleforth and seven other priests were present on the sanctuary. A full description is given of the bride's dress *"a delightful creation of ivory romaine with long train...Her tulle veil was very full and was surmounted by a dainty headdress of pearls"*. The St. Marie's boys choir was augmented by the choir from St. Charles parish and the organist was Mr Edward Hirst[72].

September - The 1937 annual retreat for the men of the parish focussed on Catholic Action and the need for the laity to become involved both politically and socially. The headline for this year's retreat was "Reading and praying are the two methods of training for Catholic Action".

The September 1938 report from the parish SVP was its 66th and contains a summary of the scale and generosity of its work. There is a word of thanks to the parish for the "bedding, clothing, books etc." donated by the parish. But the report reveals that 1,459 visits were made that year to people in need in their homes. Through these visits, 1,415 "St. Anthony's loaves"[73] were distributed. The hospitals and institutions[74] were visited and Catholic newspapers and magazines, tobacco and sweets were given to Catholic "inmates". Interestingly, the report shows that "relief" was given to "casuals" visiting the city in search of employment" and that "employment was found for several clients". Clearly devastating unemployment was still forcing men to walk to Sheffield in hope of finding work in its factories and foundries. The Jarrow March passed through Sheffield in October 1936.

October - A report is contained of the annual retreat of the Catholic Women's League.

The mosaic of St Anthony in St Marie's above the cash collection box for SVP to buy food ("St Anthony's Bread")

November - Mention is made in the 1935 magazine of *"a sparkling comedy"* called "Lucky Dip" performed at St. William's parish hall by the Sheffield Catholic Players".

December - Each year in December a *"treat"* was provided to the parish boys' choir. In 1935, as every year, they had *"a good tuck-in to turkey and plum pudding, and a visit to the pantomime"*.

Nowhere, in the 1937 or 1938 parish magazines is there any hint of unrest or concern that events unfolding in Europe might lead to another war only just over twenty years after the armistice that closed what was said to be "the war to end all wars".

---

71   Gerard Young later became a Knight of St. Gregory and was influential in developing the new church of St Francis at Crosspool.
72   The father of Mary Hirst mentioned above.
73   An expression for food parcels distributed to those in need.
74   Probably meaning both mental health institutions and the workhouses.

Chapter V
War Again, and its Aftermath 1939 – 1946

Evacuees at Sheffield station. Those with labels are leaving Sheffield

Sheffield Prepares

At 11am on Sunday 3rd September 1939, to people huddled around radios at home, the Prime Minister announced the grave news that *"this country is now at war with Germany"*. He went on to explain, *"We and France are today, in fulfilment of our obligations, going to the aid of Poland, who is so bravely resisting this wicked and unprovoked attack upon her people. We have a clear conscience – we have done all that any country could do to establish peace…I know that you will play your part with calmness and courage…May God bless you all. May he defend the right. For it is evil things we shall be fighting against – brute force, bad faith, injustice, oppression and persecution – and against them I am certain that right will prevail"*.

Few people were unaware that war was very likely. In Sheffield, as elsewhere, precautions against air raids were already in hand. Anderson shelters, made out of corrugated steel (for added strength), were being delivered to many households. It was the responsibility of the householder to dig a hole large enough to fit the shelter as delivered. Neighbours and friends worked together, in digging, bolting the sheets of metal together and then to cover the shelter with the earth dug up to form the hole within which the shelter stood.

Larger shelters were provided for schools and in some public places. Anti-aircraft guns[75], camouflaged in dug-outs, were set up in open parks and places across Sheffield. Large barrage balloons, filled with helium,

75   Known as "ack-ack" guns, from the sound they made when firing.

A family building an Anderson air-raid shelter

In Sheffield, air raid sirens were sounded 130 times during the war but, for the first 12 months, no direct attack on Sheffield took place. The first bomb fell on Sheffield during the night of 18th August 1940, and the last on 28th July 1942.

Evacuation

In cities across the country, plans were drawn up to evacuate children to safer areas in the countryside or even abroad. Sheffield, because of its importance in producing steel vital in so many ways for the war effort, was thought to be a prime target for enemy bombing.

The Sisters of Notre Dame in Sheffield soon found themselves under pressure to arrange for pupils at the girls' school to be evacuated to somewhere safer and with boarding facilities. Sister Hermingild of the Blessed Sacrament managed to find one property, well outside Sheffield, large enough but with "*manifold drawbacks*"[77]. This was Derwent Hall, the Duke Norfolk's home at Ashopthorpe to which Sheffield Catholic children as far back as 1912 had visited for a Summer treat.

In September 1939, some 150 pupils of the Cavendish Street part of the school left Sheffield under the care of the Head Mistress Sister Marie Pierre, some other sisters and four lay members of staff, Mrs Carr, Miss Hawkins, Miss Kelly and Miss Gallimore. The children whose parents did not want them to live away from home transferred to

were set up around Sheffield, each one fixed to the ground by wires, and intended to deter enemy aircraft from flying over built up areas.

At St. Marie's, Canon Bradley ceased ringing the Angelus bell, following national orders for churches to silence all bell-ringing[76]. This was because of the danger of bells being heard by enemy aircraft flying in or above low cloud and pinpointing population centres. The Angelus had been rung daily since 1865 when Canon Walshaw had introduced it, using the bell designed for that purpose dating from 1850.

Derwent Hall including St Henry's Catholic chapel

76   This ban on bell-ringing lasted until the end of the war in 1945.
77   *The Centenary of the Convent of Notre Dame, Sheffield 1855 -1955,* unattributed author, page 10.

The interior of the chapel at Derwent Hall

building called Derwent Hall, built in 1672, totally unsuitable to be a school…It must have been an absolute nightmare to organize, as everything had to be transported from Sheffield – chairs, tables, desks, crockery, blackboards, piano etc…There was no hot water until a boiler could be installed, and then only four bath cubicles were made. Four baths for over 150 bodies… Didn't worry us though!…

"So now I had to get used to living with a whole lot of other people, instead of with just my own family[81]. I acquired two new friends, Bernadette Gregory and Agnes McDermott, two lovely Irish Catholic girls, who were just as mad as I was and we formed a committed 'Unholy Trio…

"In the mornings, because it was still a Convent, all the Catholic girls had to get up and be ready for 6.00am prayers. I, being a non-Catholic, had the luxury of

the safer Oakbrook site despite the somewhat crowded conditions this caused[78].

One pupil who was evacuated to Derwent Hall contributed her memories to a BBC history archive in 2003[79]. She and her sister were originally due to be evacuated to Australia to live with an uncle's family, through the British government's evacuation project run by "The Children's Overseas Reception Board". She writes:

"Plans went ahead and we had our injections and got passports. We were allowed to take one suitcase of clothes and toys…We had everything together, and were ready to go, when there was a dreadful tragedy at sea. A whole ship full of children being evacuated was bombed and sunk, with no survivors…[80]

"However the school came up with another plan. They would evacuate the whole school out into the Derbyshire countryside…There was a large, old, rambling stone

The June 1940 First Holy Communion group at Derwent Hall.
Left to right starting at the top: John Sawtell,
Phillipa Darley, Leonie McDonagh, Margaret Westmoreland,
Peter Granelli and Paul Huntingdon

78   Ibid p.10.
79   www.bbc.co.uk/history/ww2peopleswar/stories.shtml
80   This was probably the SS. City of Benares, a steam passenger ship bound for Canada with 90 children on board. It was travelling in convoy but was torpedoed by the Germans 253 miles out in the Atlantic. 77 of the children and 183 adults were killed in the attack. It was not the case that there were no survivors.
81   It seems that this boarder joined the school in September 1940, one year into the evacuation. This would tie in the date of evacuation given in the school centenary booklet, the change of plans because of the Benares tragedy and her making new friends because it seems she was a new girl.

25

staying in bed another half hour...As there was no heating whatsoever in the whole building, there were many moans as warm bodies hit cold air and, even worse, cold water...

"Several nuns were very kind to us, but they were really out of their depth in having to control children twenty-four hours a day. They were used to an ordered life which ended when school was finished for the day, and they could retire to the peace of their nunnery. This was the reason, I imagine, for the 6.30pm bed rule".

The nuns themselves recorded[82]

"For nearly two years, at the cost of heroic efforts on the part of all, a practically full time programme of educational work was maintained at Derwent Hall, whilst so many schools were closed or functioning part time only. However, by May 1941, the living conditions had deteriorated to such an extent that the parents were informed that it would be impossible to continue after 31st July".

With the Cavendish Street school site very much under-used during the evacuation, attempts were made to requisition it for other purposes. To avoid this, the Sister Superior wisely had air raid shelters built so that the remaining children, not able to go either to Derwent or to Fulwood, could be taught (in the event of an air raid warning) inside the shelters that were deliberately large enough to act as classrooms.

By September 1941, the whole school was reunited on its two sites for the remainder of the war and thereafter.

Many other children, too, though evacuated for safety, returned to Sheffield within a month or two as no air raids came and separation proved too much.

Notre Dame schoolgirl evacuees at Derwent Hall

82   *The Centenary of the Convent of Notre Dame Sheffield. p.10.*

The saving of the stained glass of St. Marie's (Part 1)[83]

In 1939, Cecil Higgins was an employee of Robertson and Russell Ltd, a manufacturer of stained glass whose offices were in Carver Street, next to St. Matthew's church. When war broke out, Sheffield was expected to become a major target for German bombing, additionally so because of its large scale manufacturing of armaments. In the Autumn of 1939, the Provost of Sheffield, the Very Rev. Alfred Jarvis, engaged Robertson and Russell Ltd to remove and store in a safe place all the major stained glass windows of the churches of the Diocese of Sheffield. It was Cecil Higgins who was deputed by his employer to travel around the diocese removing and storing the windows selected by each vicar. When Roman Catholic priests also approached him to have their glass protected, he agreed to this. For efficiency in this time-restricted task[84], Cecil included nearby Catholic churches as he made his way, with a team of about twelve men, to the parish churches across the diocese. Hence St. Marie's glass was protected early on and immediately after Sheffield's Anglican cathedral had been attended to.

Two methods of protecting church windows were used. If the window was considered valuable or special and was robust enough to be removed in sections, Cecil made sketches of each window and its inscriptions, taking care to record how all the individual sections removed would fit back together. For smaller or more fragile windows, the technique used was to board up the window both inside and out and then pour in sand on both sides, between the boarding and the glass, to hold the glass secure against any bomb blast. When he met Canon Bradley at St. Marie's, the canon was keen that the East window, the West window and the Canon Dolan memorial window should be removed for safe storage.

Far too much glass was recovered for storage at the Carver Street premises, which, in any case, would have been under as much danger of bombing as the nearby churches. So Cecil Higgins approached a local coal mine[85] to store the glass.

Cecil Higgins recalls riding on a bogey with two miners to see where the wooden crates containing the window sections would be placed. Alarmed at seeing ripples on water in the gloom as they drove, he was assured by the miners that whilst that part of the mine was flooded, the place intended for the storage was above this. As extra assurance he was told that a pump worked continuously, drawing water off for use by the coke ovens at Handsworth. In the haste to get on with the storage and to move on to other places, Cecil recalls how there wasn't time to argue. To save time he also agreed that storage would be at the owner's own risk. However, just in case of later flooding, Cecil made sure that the sketches and instructions for reconstruction for each of the windows were safely sealed inside watertight cylinders placed inside each crate[86].

The Sheffield Blitz

Bombers had targeted Sheffield with minor sorties from August 1940, but it was suspected that these were more important to the enemy as reconnaissance missions. Coventry and Birmingham had both suffered *blitzkrieg*. Sheffield, it was widely believed, would be next.

On the two nights of 12/13th and 15/16thDecember 1940, Sheffield suffered its own blitz[87]. Over 330 German aircraft dropped some 350 tonnes of high explosives in 1,200 bombs and parachute mines, together with over 16,000 incendiary canisters designed to burn buildings to the ground. In these two nights, 668 Sheffield civilians and 25 service personnel were killed and 1,586 people were injured. Over 82,000 houses were either damaged or destroyed - almost half the total number of houses in the city. Thousands were made homeless.

The air-raid sirens sounded shortly before 7 o'clock in the evening of 12th December on a clear moonlit night. Flares and incendiary bombs dropped from aircraft lit up the city centre. The industrial areas to the East were covered by fog. The path of the planes and the line of destruction was from the South West, with bombs hitting

Blitz damage near St Mary's Road

---

83   The story of the saving of the windows of St. Marie's comes directly from an interview with Cecil Higgins, in 2003.

84   His employer had no idea how long it would be before Mr Higgins and other younger employees would be called up for military service, so speed was considered important.

85   Nunnery Colliery at Handswoth. This mine was owned by the Duke of Norfolk. It seems that this was the only site chosen for the St.Marie's windows alone, perhaps because the Duke permitted free or less expensive storage there.

86   For Part Two of the story of the saving of St. Marie's glass, see page 32 below.

87   Figures from www.sheffiledhistory.co.uk/forum/index/topic/the story of the Sheffield blitz; Sources for the Study of the Sheffield Blitz of 1940,Sheffield City Council; and BBC.co.uk/ww2peopleswar/stories

Norton Lees, Gleadless, Abbeydale, onwards to the city centre and spreading to Walkley, Broomhill, Owlerton, Meersbrook and Wybourn. The bombardment went on for 9 hours. Over 100 bombs fell within the parish of St. Marie's, with major devastation also in the surrounding parishes of St. Wilfrid's, St. Vincent's and St. Catherine's.

St. Marie's Girl's School in St. Mary's Road was among the eight Sheffield schools that were bombed and destroyed that night.

The Women's Voluntary Service providing tea near St. Mary's Road after the blitz

Many of the children had been evacuated to Melton Mowbray on September 1st – the day Hitler invaded Poland. The children had marched along Suffolk Road to the station with teachers and many parents who had come to say goodbye. That was months before St. Marie's Girls' School, the oldest Catholic girls' school in the city, was destroyed by the blast from a land mine dropped on the nearby goods station. A member of staff, Miss Hazel Worth, came to the rubble the next day and rescued as many books and as much equipment as possible. What could be saved was stored for safe keeping in the Parish Room at St. Marie's. The staff room and everything in it, as well as the piano from the infant department, had been destroyed. Further efforts to find and recover whatever could be were halted when police arrived to announce an unexploded bomb nearby. Everyone had to leave.

When school recommenced it was achieved by the girls moving into the ground floor of St. Marie's Boys School. Space became very tight. A further burden was that the school had no air raid shelter and so everyone had to be drilled weekly in practice evacuations to the public shelters at Duchess Road. No air raids came but, it was recorded, the practices provided fun for the children and hassle for the teachers.

Much closer to St. Marie's, Walsh's store was badly damaged. At around 10.50pm, C and A Modes on High Street was blown apart by a direct hit.

A tram ablaze outside C and A Modes

The tailors Montague Burton, at the top of Angel Street, was burnt to the ground[88]. Also close to St. Marie's that night, an unknown number of people, believed to be between 70 and 80, took shelter in the Marples Hotel on the corner of Fitzalan Square, a seven storey building. At the height of the blitz they all went down into the cellar for safety. At 11.44pm Marples took a direct hit and the whole building collapsed into "a 15 foot high mound of rubble". Only seven people survived and only 14 bodies were ever recovered and identified. Unidentified remains recovered were later interred in the mass grave at City Road Cemetery where 134 victims of that night are buried. The 1,000 tons of rubble that was Marples Hotel was eventually cleared but the site is known still to contain many bodies.

The remains of Marples Hotel (foreground)

Peter Lodge[89], then a five year old parishioner, remembers his father[90] coming home to Crosspool that night after co-ordinating rescues in Norton. Later that evening they

---

88 One employee reported [www.sheffieldhistory.co.uk/forums/index/topic/69 the-story-of-the-Sheffield-blitz] how he walked to work the next morning amid bodies laid out in the street, rubble and broken glass everywhere and broken water mains gushing water.

89 Interviewed in June 2016 at his home, together with Bryan Beedham.

90 Who, the previous week had been passed as "A1" fit to join the army but, at that time, had a reserved occupation as a co-ordinator of rescue and rebuilding for the City Council.

A Crosspool house bombed
(possibly the same house as was near Peter Lodge's home)

heard a dull thump and then a flapping sound. Peter's father instantly recognizing the sound as a parachute bomb landing very close by, its silk parachute blowing in the wind and its fuse about to detonate. He "threw" Peter and his mother under the kitchen table. Moments later the house shook and the front door was sucked off its hinges. A house in the road opposite was half gone, its roof blown off. The occupants, a family of three, killed in the blast. Peter remembers standing looking through the gap that was his front door, and seeing Sheffield burning in the darkness far below. His mother was acutely aware that people in Crosspool had not been issued with Anderson shelters where others across the city had been.

Bryan Beedham, Peter's friend, lived at Norton Lees in 1940. That evening his father was on duty in the Home Guard. His mother, his sister and he were making and putting up Christmas decorations. They hadn't heard the warning siren. His mother asked him to go outside and fetch the step ladder so she could hang the streamers. He couldn't believe his eyes. A nearby wood was ablaze. A plane, he now believes, had crashed and set it alight. His mother ran out and together they saw Sheffield ablaze. One of the first incendiary bombs hit Lavers, the timber yard, at the bottom of the Moor. They could see it. They ran to their Anderson shelter, terrified. They finally slept soundly and were only awakened by a Home Guard concerned that they had not been seen after the "All Clear" siren. Bryan's father was still at work amid the devastation.

Three days later, a second night of bombing came with over 100 enemy aircraft. This time they did hit steelworks, industrial sites and yet more houses in Attercliffe, Grimesthorpe and Burngreave. Peter Lodge believes the chief target was the River Don works where the crankshafts for Spitfire, Hurricane and Lancaster planes were manufactured.

On the morning after each bombardment, bodies were laid in the streets, buildings continued to burn or smoulder, and debris was everywhere. In St. Mary's Road, very near where the parish girls' school had stood, "all the houses on both sides of the road" burned. Among the families in the area was the family of James (Bobbie)

Bryan Beedham's painting of the height of the Sheffield Blitz in High Street

Walsh[91], his wife Elizabeth and their children Frances, Mary, Alice and Leo. Alice remembers it well.

Another parishoner recalls coming to Mass on the Sunday morning picking her way through rubble the whole length of the Moor. On the Moor, all the shops near the top of the street had been bombed and were still on fire. Whole rows of buildings were gone. She remembers, too, another Catholic family moving in to her family's home in Norfolk Road the day following the second raid and a policeman ordering them all out of the house when an unexploded bomb was found next door. They all had to spend several nights in a reception centre in Arbourthorne, with meals provided by the Women's Royal Voluntary Service. After that her family was housed, for a while, with a family in Totley.

St. Marie's had escaped major damage. But the two side windows in the Blessed Sacrament Chapel had been blown in and destroyed in the blitz, some say burned by the heat of the sugar burning in Tuckwood's bakery nearby. It is not known whether these and other smaller stained glass windows at St. Marie's had been boarded up. It is reported that St. Marie's was very gloomy during the war years (possibly because of lower windows being boarded up), but the fact that the small tracery glass within the Blessed Sacrament Chapel windows did survive suggests that the larger glass areas were insufficiently protected with boarding.

Following the two major attacks of December 1940, Sheffield did not suffer blitzkrieg again. The focus of German air power shifted as new fronts opened in Europe. The Battle of Britain had been won. But Sheffield's Blitz had taken the lives of 668 civilians, of whom some 25% had addresses within the boundaries of the parish as it then was. How many were Catholic parishioners has not been researched.

Parish Life During the War

The routines of parish life at St. Marie's throughout World War II continued as closely as possible to the pre-war years. Petrol rationing reduced a range of occasional activities. Mary Hirst[92] recalls that the annual choir competition, organised through the Notre Dame Catholic Teacher Training College in Manchester and held there, had to cease. This was particularly a disappointment because St. Marie's school choir had been prominent in the competition for the singing of plainchant. A special

uniform was worn, made by parents in a blue material. Mary recalls how some parents from the St. Oswald's area were unable to afford the uniform, so their girls stood out, wearing other clothes.

Another annual event that ceased was the Summer Harvest camp in Lincolnshire, organized by Fr. Morgan Sweeney, the priest son of the Sweeney family who lived at Claywood Road. Winifred Sweeney was Mary Hirst's best friend. Together they helped with the cooking for the boys at the camp whom Fr. Sweeney brought from the poorer parts of Bradford. Most days, the two girls would also help with the harvest work.

Gone, too, were the parish charabanc trips to the seaside at Cleethorpes for both the choir and servers.

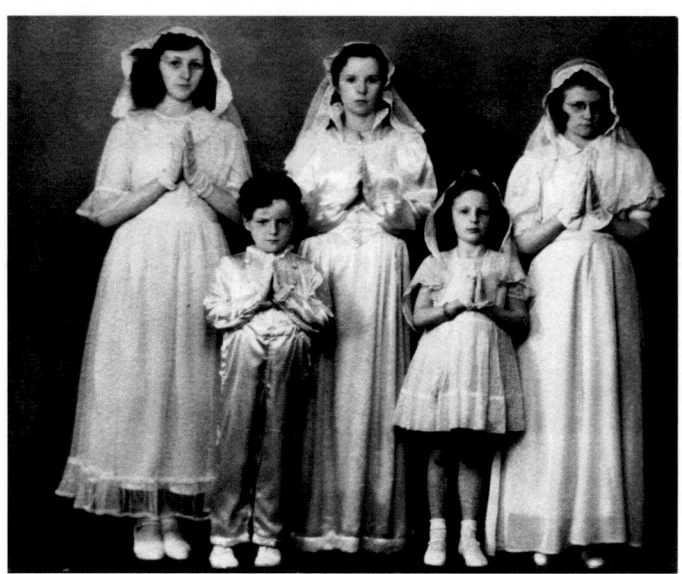

1943 May Queen Mary Cull with two attendants, a page boy (John Cull) and Hazel Leach (cushion bearer)

Throughout the war, Sunday morning Masses were unchanged. The 9.45am Children's Mass saw all the children in the front rows, girls on the "Gospel" side and boys on the "Epistle" side[93]. A nun from school sat at the end of each pew, helping to file the children in orderly fashion to Holy Communion before the rest of the parish, which included their parents, were able to come forward.

Every Sunday, from 1940 until 1945, after the Children's Mass, tea was provided free of charge to all servicemen. Mary Hirst would help her mother, Laura, her aunt Agnes[94] and a Mrs Woulfe to set up tables and chairs. Some of the wounded servicemen from Middlewood Hospital, in their blue uniforms, regularly attended.

---

91   His nickname was acquired because he was a policeman.

92   Born in 1928, her father, Edward, was the organist at St. Marie's for some 50 years.

93   The priest would read the Epistle at the altar (in Latin) from the Missal at one side of the altar. The book was then moved by the server to the other end of the altar for the reading of the Gospel. At St. Marie's, the gospel side of the altar would be the end closer to the Blessed Sacrament chapel.

94   Agnes was Edward Hirst's sister. She could remember seeing Queen Victoria, in 1897, in her carriage as she was driven from Sheffield station to the Duke of Norfolk's property in Norfolk Park. Aunt Agnes had pink gloves bought for her for the occasion from Walsh's department store, later to become House of Fraser and , then, T.J. Hughes store.

But evening meetings and services[95] in winter were brought forward to finish by 4pm to enable everyone to get home before dark, because of 'the blackout'. The 'blackout' prohibited all lights, whether street lighting or lights within buildings that did not have thick blackout curtains. Wardens patrolled streets to ensure that the 'blackout' orders were obeyed. School times, too, were changed. Whenever the air-raid 'all-clear' siren was sounded after 1am, school would remain closed until 10am, giving time for uninterrupted sleep in bed following the cramped and fear-filled hours sitting awake in an air raid shelter.

Victory and Returning From War

On 8th May 1945 the war in Europe was over. The drabness, shortages and on-going rationing were forgotten as bunting appeared and celebrations and street parties were held all across the city. Close to St. Marie's, the Star newspaper building was bedecked with bunting and flags and crowds filled the streets. The pubs and the new milk bar in Pinstone Street (a new concept brought straight from London by Mr Marsden, using milk and ice cream from his Sandygate Dairy), all did a roaring trade.

But there were also the memories of those who would not be coming home, killed in the many theatres of war over almost six years of conflict on land, at sea and in the air. And it is an immense shame that there seems to be no record of the men and women of St. Marie's parish who lost their lives in active service in World War II. This is in sharp contrast to the care that Canon Dolan had shown in his efforts to ensure that the community should not forget the parishioners who perished in World War I.

One parishioner who did return from wartime service was John Maher who, for many years before his death in 2006, proudly kept alive the commemoration at St. Marie's, each November, of those who had died in both World Wars. A prisoner of war, captured from the sea off Singapore, John endured the barbarity and appalling conditions of Japanese POW camps and was used as forced labour to build the infamous Railway of Death and the Bridge over the River Kwai[96].

A Victory parade in Fargate, 1945

95   Mass was not celebrated after midday because of the obligation to fast from the previous evening before receiving Holy Communion.

96   Appendix Two gives detail of John's wartime life and his subsequent contribution to the life of the parish.

Another returning parishioner was Cyril Morewood who, after the D Day landings, was among those who fought their way across northern France and into Belgium where, at a rural farm, he met his future wife, Justine. Eventually husband and wife returned to Sheffield and endured the harshness of inadequate housing until the slum clearances around Duke Street and the eventual freedom of a home in temporary housing in the Norfolk Park area[97]. After the war Cyril became friends with Billy Lund who had also found and married a Belgian wife in the closing phase of the war. Billy had spent much of the war at sea on Arctic patrols and convoy protection.

The Saving of the Stained Glass Windows of St. Marie's (Part 2)[98]

Having served in the North African campaign, then in Italy and eventually in Germany, Cecil Higgins[99] returned to his former employment in 1946. He was immediately called on to reinstate windows into the churches from which they had been taken. For the St. Marie's windows, he went back to the Nunnery Colliery where he had stored them in 1940. To his horror, he found that the water level in the mine had risen considerably, drowning the gallery in which he had stacked the crates of stained glass. Early in the war, the pump controlling the water level in the mine had broken and had not been repaired. The agreement had been that the glass would be stored at the owners' own risk. The crates had been under water for five years.

What Mr Higgins found was only mud. The wooden crates had rotted through. The glass had come loose from the lead and sunk as individual fragments into the grey mud, twelve inches deep.

Not one of the water-tight cylinders containing his sketches and notes on how to reconstruct each window was to be found. Presumably, freed from the rotting crates, they had floated away to somewhere in the mine. The second copy of the drawings and notes had been destroyed when his employers' offices in Carver Street was destroyed in the Sheffield Blitz. Mr Higgins recalled going to see Canon Bradley for the only remaining copy so that he could return the windows to St. Marie's.

"And so I came here . I came in the door I've come in today and I was shown into Canon Bradley's room and he was sat back in a low chair. There were newspapers all around him – he'd let them drop to the floor. So I said, 'Good afternoon'. So he looked at me. 'Should I know you?', he said. 'How did you get in here?' I said,

'I've come through the front door'. And so, believe it or not, he looked at me as if he'd never seen me in his life before. So I said, 'Well, I've come about your stained glass'. So he stood up, straightened himself, knocked some cigarette ash off the front of him and then he says, 'Ah. Are you going to do it then?'. I says, 'Yes I'm going to put it back. You do want it put back?'. He says, 'Of course I do. That's why I phoned you up'. So I said, 'Well, I've come to see if you've got your copy of all the windows that were taken out that I gave you'. 'Oh', he says, 'There's been six years of war. Didn't you know about that?'. I said, 'I know about it all right. I've been in the army... But' I said, 'I want those now because they've all been lost in the colliery. There's none there'. So he says, 'Well, I haven't got any'. I looked at him and said, 'You what?'. He says, 'I haven't got any. If you took 'em out, it's your responsibility. You see that they're put back. If you know your job, that's your job'. So I thought, 'Well. That's it!'"[100]

For six weeks, Cecil Higgins sorted through thousands of pieces of glass from the West window, struggling to make sense of the images. Then he raised the reconstructed panels into place with temporary fixings and called on Canon Bradley to confirm that the design was correct. Viewing the window through opera glasses, the Canon disagreed. He insisted that two tiny pieces of glass at the apex of the window were the wrong way round. Cecil insisted they couldn't be since to turn them round would place the painted surface on the exterior of the building, contrary to glazing norms. The two men could not agree on this. Mr Higgins challenged him to explain why he was so sure of the error. The interview records:

"Then he [Canon Bradley] felt inside his cassock and brought out a book....the frontispiece inside, when he opened it, was a full page colour representation of that window...I says to him, 'Have you had that all the time?'. 'Yes I have.'...I says, 'Why didn't you tell me? I've had to do all this from memory'. He says, 'Well I wanted to see how well you knew your job'. I says, 'Well I'll tell you how well I know my job – it's going to cost you another £600, that!'"

Ted Cummings, a parishioner of St. Vincent's parish, who had joined us part way through the interview with Mr. Higgins, recalled how he and a friend had been asked by Canon Bradley soon afterwards to make a door-to-door collection around the parish in an attempt to raise the extra money now needed to pay for the restoration of the windows.

---

97   Cyril and Justine later moved to their own home within the parish where, along with his wife, Cyril celebrated his 100th birthday a few days before the end of 2016.

98   Appendix Three is a transcript of the key parts of the wide-ranging interview that, among wider matters, gave detail of both the removal of the windows and their rescue and re-construction by him in 1946. Cecil Higgins died, aged 104 in February 2017.

99   The employee of Robertson and Russell who had removed the major windows of St Marie's and stored them in a mine.

100   The 2003 interview with Cecil Higgins took place in the Parish Room at St Marie's, adjoining the Presbytery.

Chapter VI
The Post-War Parish 1946 - 1950

A 1949 class photograph outside St Marie's school

From the Parish Magazines

The *St. Marie's Catholic Monthly* for 1946 and 1947 show how little parish life had changed in the previous ten years that had included World War II. The guilds and sodalities remained much the same. Though the St. Marie's Wolf Cubs and Boy Scouts seem to have gone, a new St. Marie's Youth Club had been started. Miss Hazel Worth, a teacher at St. Marie's school, had formed a youth club during the war that met on Wednesday and Friday evenings in the Parish Room. Among the activities provided were Bank Holiday walks in Derbyshire, various games and craftwork and (in the sacristy) mending vestments, cottas and replacing buttons onto altar servers' cassocks[101].

Two other new Catholic groups were the Legion of Mary and the Catholic Social Guild, founded to promote Catholic Social Teaching. Its 1946 entry in the parish magazine reports that, following the exhortation of Pope Leo XIII fifty six years before that miners and quarrymen

be given shorter working weeks due to the severity of their labour, the British government had finally approved a five day working week for miners from 1st May. The July 1947 edition records another socially focussed group being formed to support and encourage those struggling to improve employment conditions, namely the Association of Catholic Trade Unionists.

The tone of the themes for the January week of prayer for Christian unity and the Lenten Pastoral Letter belie harsh attitudes and the perceived necessity of all others to abandon their faith and traditions and return to visible unity as Catholics.

In July 1946, as part of a world-wide examination of the lived faith of the Church, a petition to Rome was received. Parishioners (who agreed) were invited to sign. It sought to find out the belief of Catholics on the Assumption of Our Lady. Pope Pius XII was considering declaring this as a dogma of the Church and was confirming the belief of the Church universally. The petition read,

---

101   Miss Hirst (daughter of Edward Hirst, the organist and choirmaster at St. Marie's from the early 1930s until the 1960s) recalls that the sacristan, George Evinson, was an untidy person which seemed to annoy Miss Worth.

"We the under-signed do firmly believe that God, not allowing the most pure body of the Virgin Mother to see corruption, by special privilege, raised her up from the dead, so that now she reigns for ever in heaven...We earnestly pray that the doctrine of the bodily Assumption of Our Blessed Lady Mary...be defined as a dogma of faith".

Three years later, at the conclusion of this testing of Catholic faith, the Assumption was declared a part of Catholic belief.

The November 1946 accounts of St. Marie's Society of St. Vincent de Paul, published in the parish magazine, shows an annual spend of £381[102], of which £147 was given in bread and groceries, £11 in clothing and a further £147 as cash grants to the poor. The accounts of the following year show that 1,165 home visits had been made, 166 visit to institutions for the old, infirm or mentally ill and parcels sent to the Lodge Moor Prisoner of War camp[103].

On Low Sunday 1947, a parishioner of St. Marie's, Lawrence Waller, was ordained priest at Leeds Cathedral. Fr. Waller followed in the footsteps of others from the parish who had been ordained, notably, Fr. Rowland Broomhead, Fr. Samuel Sayles, four of the sons of Dr. Arnold Knight, Fr. Thomas Eyre, Fr. William Hayes whose family ran the Dog and Partridge public house, Fr. Morgan Sweeney and, of course, Canon Bradley.

Summer 1947 records successes in Notre Dame school's religious education examinations. 44 girls were awarded the Certificate of RE and all 25 who attempted the Higher Certificate were successful.

The December 1947 edition of *St Marie's Catholic Monthly* lists the donors to the on-going collection to pay off the cost of restoring the stained glass windows.

The Polish Community at St. Marie's

In 1945, when World War II in Europe ended, tens of thousands of Polish soldiers, who had fought with the allies found themselves unable to return home to Poland. Civilians too, who had fled to England, were in the same position. Their homeland was free from Nazi aggression yet was now suffering under Soviet aggression and occupation. The freedom and independence for which Poles had fought fiercely was never granted. The allied Yalta agreement ceded Poland to Stalin's Russia. The war had begun with Nazi Germany invading Poland and ended with Communist Russia already in occupation. In 1939, Hitler had ordered that the standard of living in Poland be kept low, that Polish intellectuals be eliminated and that the population be used as a source of forced labour in Germany. By 1945 there were 3.5 million Polish workers in Germany in this category. In 1940 Stalin had similar plans and ordered mass deportations of Poles to Uzbekistan and Kurdistan. A further 1.5 million men were sent to camps in Siberia.

In 1941, the Polish government in exile in London successfully proposed to Stalin that, with Britain now an ally and in need of larger forces, a Polish army could be raised for Britain made up of men released from Russian captivity. Over 100,000 released Poles reached evacuation camps on the Caspian Sea and were taken to Persia (later Iran) and then on to Egypt where many formed a Polish corps in the British 8th Army fighting in North Africa. It was largely these men who, in 1945 after four years of fighting for the allies, found their way to Britain.

Additionally, in 1939, a Polish army was formed of Poles fleeing west to Britain. Many, too, joined the RAF and fought in the Battle of Britain, accounting for 15% of all Germany's losses in that crucial battle. But wherever Polish forces fought, it was the Poles who suffered the heaviest percentage losses within the allied forces, perhaps due to their tenacity and determination against the Nazi force that was destroying their country.

In 1946, large numbers of Poles first arrived in Sheffield. These were mainly men serving on shell and bomb clearance who were being demobilized. Because of serious shortages in housing, initially Polish ex-soldiers were billeted in the now disused prisoner of war camps such as those at Malin Bridge and at High Green[104]. Over much of Britain, the POW camps were often far from places to work and earn money in order to begin a new life. But in Sheffield employment prospects were good because of a thriving engineering and metal working industry, the steel works and a major need for labourers to repair or rebuild war-damaged housing. Forty eight percent of Polish immigrant men went into the steel works and were soon able to move nearer to their workplaces, gravitating to the poorer districts of Brightside and Attercliffe, where landladies were said to accept new tenants, cramming men in as many as five in a room[105]. During 1946 and 1947, 1200 former soldiers and Polish refugees settled in Sheffield. Most were alone and many had families either in Poland or still in refugee camps in Palestine, Lebanon, North Africa and India. A further 300 Poles had arrived as refugees from the displaced persons' camps in Germany.

---

102   £14,400 in 2016 terms.
103   Which by then may have been used to house Polish ex-soldiers and airmen.
104   Anna Kucewicz, *The Immigrant Experience: The Reception of Polish Refugees and their Adaptation to Life in Sheffield Post 1945.* p. 32.
105   Ibid p.44.

The 1947 Polish Resettlement Act eased the position of the ex-servicemen and political refugees, helping towards their being able to bring their wives and children to Britain. Slowly at first, the number of Polish Catholics living in Sheffield increased. Families were re-united, single men brought girl friends or fiancés to join them in England and more people from displaced persons' camps in Germany found freedom. By the end of 1948, the Polish Mass at St. Marie's, celebrated with the cooperation of Canon Bradley, was attracting an increasing number of Poles.

During the war, Poles serving in the allied forces had been strongly nationalist and independent, establishing Polish newspapers with Polish journalists for Polish troops. Now the war was over and with new challenges facing them, they often found their own solutions, not relying on anyone else. This approach usually involved working closely together and so bonded and strengthened the Polish community. For example, to the exploitation by Sheffield landlords charging high rent for poor housing, the response was to establish a Polish hostel for men. When their families began to arrive from 1948, even though free education was provided in state schools, the Polish community quickly established a Saturday school for Polish children. This was seen as crucial to maintaining Polish identity, providing, as it did, a Polish environment where Polish children could be taught in their own language, could learn of their own history, culture and heritage, enjoy national dances, songs and literature and, on special occasions, wear their own national costume. The Saturday school, established in 1950 initially as a nursery run from St. Marie's parish hall, was staffed by volunteers from within the Sheffield Polish community.

Fr. Michal Szymankiewicz, the first Polish priest in Sheffield and founder of the Polish mission, arrived in 1946. He was a key influence in the project to form a Polish school and became one of its first teachers. When pupils exceeded 35, the school moved to the already established Polish YMCA premises. In 1953 the school became an independent organization under, at first, the Polish Combatants Association and, later, under the Polish Education Society. In 1954 the Polish school was able to use the premises of the Polish Ex--Servicemen's Association established in Sheffield that year[106]. Through the efforts of Fr. Szymankiewicz, the school was able to use, for a while, the premises and equipment of a local English school in Pomona Street and then at Hunter's Bar, eventually settling, in 1963, at the new Polish Parish Centre on Ecclesall Road. By this time the

The Polish school in the 1950s gathered aroun Father Michal Szymankiewicz

106   In 1946 Branch No 439 of the Ex-Servicemen's Association was set up in Wood Lane Camp, Stannington by the Polish troops billeted there. The Association's statutes, drawn up in London, were political in nature, with long term aims to preserve Polish cultural values and to resist the assimilation of Poles into British culture that risked loss of national identity among those in exile.

After a Polish School performance

school comprised a nursery, four primary classes and a secondary class assisting young people to prepare for O-level exams in Polish as a second language [107].

Fr. Michal Szymankiewicz was ordained a priest in 1938 at Vilnius, then part of Poland. As a young priest he worked in a parish in the East of Poland (later absorbed into Belarus). In 1940 he moved to Lithuania possibly to escape Soviet forces. In June 1941 he was arrested by the Communist Secret Police in the mass deportations from Lithuania. He was sent to north-eastern Russia where he continued his priestly work secretly among the exiles. Later that year, under an amnesty (probably linked to the formation of new forces to fight for the allies) Fr. Szymankiewicz joined a new Polish army as a chaplain in Uzbekistan. From here he went with the Polish forces

Preparing for a Polish Corpus Christi procession in the 1960s

107   The Polish Saturday School continues to this day, with the 65th anniversary of opening being passed in 2015. Its history is summarized in *65 Years of Polish Education in Sheffield* privately published and from which details have been drawn.

Fr Szymankiewicz leads the Polish War Memorial Service outside the City Hall 10th September 1966

to Iran, staying with the troops as they fought through the Middle East, in North Africa and eventually in Italy and Germany. After the war he came to England and became chaplain to Polish troops including those at Potter Hill in High Green, before working from St. Marie's[108].

For many years the centre for social life, for both the Polish parish and the Polish Ex-Servicemen's Association (SPK) was the Polish YMCA first in Pitsmoor and, later, in Attercliffe. Here the Saturday school, a Polish library, the welfare club and the Polish choir, as well as other activities all thrived. Periodically events and performances were organized at the City Hall which enabled Polish culture to be seen in dance, craftwork, singing and literature and, each November, Polish Independence Day and Remembrance Day were celebrated solemnly and with dignity.

But it took until 1954 to obtain City Council permission to open SPK club premises in Dover Road. It then took a further nine years for a centre for the Polish parish to be built on Ecclesall Road. From 1963 the Polish Ex-Servicemen's Association and the Polish parish could operate almost adjacent to each other, emphasising the continuing close bond between the Polish parish and Polish nationalism.

The dedication of the icon of
Our Lady of Częstochowa in St. Marie's

108   After many years of service to Sheffield's Polish community, Fr. Szymankiewicz died suddenly in 1979 and was buried at City Road cemetery. cf: *65 Years of Polish Education in Sheffield* p.29.

Chapter VII
Into a Second Century
– St. Marie's 1950 to1960

Centenary Celebrations

The few remaining copies of *St. Marie's Catholic Monthly* magazine of 1950 show a parish proud of its history and ready to celebrate. The post war years across Britain were plain, economically restrained and low on both reasons and funds to celebrate. Nationally, the Royal Wedding of 1947 and the Coronation of 1953 were high points amid years of only slow return to prosperity. Over several monthly editions, the parish magazine carried articles covering the history of the parish and its schools. By the end of August the appeal for funds for the centenary celebrations had reached one thousand, eight hundred and two pounds, thirteen shillings and "thru-pence[109]" . The austerity of the times makes this achievement remarkable and an indicator of the strong ties felt towards this church.

On 2nd September, the centenary month, an octave[110] of prayer began and contained the principle centenary celebration[111]. The octave included:

Day 1   a Requiem Mass for Fr. Charles Pratt, founder of St. Marie's;

Day 2   Pontifical High Mass;

Day 3   Mass for all deceased priests who had served at St. Marie's;

Day 4   Mass for all benefactors who had contributed to St. Marie's;

Day 5   Mass for choristers and church workers;

Day 6   Mass for teachers at the schools of the parish;

Day 7   Mass for the Altar Society and other confraternities of the parish;

Day 8   Mass for all deceased parishioners.

Sheffield Telegraph on Monday 4th September carried details of the centenary Mass and the celebratory luncheon of the previous day. Even before the Pontifical Mass at 11.15am, it reported, "*no fewer than eight services*" had taken place in St. Marie's[112]. Despite seats at the Pontifical Mass being allocated beforehand, "*a long queue*" of people wanting to enter the church had formed in Norfolk Row.

The procession in Norfolk Row showing Bishop George Brunner, Auxiliary Bishop of Middlesborough, Frs. J Dignam and M.V. Sweeney with servers Wilfred Doyle, Gerald Tyrell and Mark Hodges

Bishop George Brunner, Auxiliary Bishop of Middlesbrough, celebrated the Mass since Leeds Diocese was awaiting the appointment of a bishop following the death of Bishop Poskitt the previous February. Monsignor John Dinn, the Administrator of Leeds Cathedral assisted Bishop Brunner. Also present and listed by *Sheffield Telegraph* were priests born in the parish – "*Very Rev. J. Dignam, Rector of Mount St. Mary's College, Spinkhill, near Sheffield, who preached at the evening service and Fr. M.V. Sweeney, headmaster of St. Bede's Grammar School, Bradford*".

109   More than £58,000 at 2017 prices.
110   Eight days.
111   Though September 11th was the actual centenary of the opening, circumstances prevented the main celebration on that date. Instead this took place on September 3rd.
112   These would have included Masses said at side altars (some simultaneously) by priests who would later attend the Pontifical Mass. Concelebration of Mass was introduced into the Church only in the 1960s.

The St. Marie's bells were peeled by the parish ringers lead by Mr. H. Hurst with *"touches of bob major and grand-sire triples before and after the morning and evening services"*. The choir comprised *"16 past and present choristers whose length of service totals over 500 years"*.

St. Marie's bellringers in the belfry loft around 1952. Left to right back row: Leslie Leach, Frank (?), bell captain Harry Hurst, Denis Baines, Valerie Leach (later Sr. Bernardette SND). Front: Julia Hirst (who later entered Carmel), Hazel Leach and Annette Milner.

"The eminent Catholic divine" Monsignor Ronald Knox preached. In his sermon he referred to the building and the Catholic life of its parishioners. *"A hundred years ago"*, he told the congregation, St. Marie's *"was the newest of 61 churches in the Yorkshire District. Now it is one of the oldest among the 360 churches in the two dioceses of Leeds and Middlesbrough"*[113].

He went on to link the building of St. Marie's to its long spiritual life. *"This building typifies, in the first instance, the age-long permanence of the Catholic Church; all the more readily because, by happy accident, the year it was raised was the year in which the English hierarchy was restored. Or, again, it records the continuous life of a single parish; a hundred years of patient witness to the Christian faith, here in the heart of a great city. Or, finally, it may make us think of the multitudinous obscure lives that were lived in the shadow of this Church, and drew from it the sacramental strength that went with them on their journey. How many have been regenerated at that font; how many secrets, never repeated to human ears, have been whispered through the grills of those confessionals; what multitude have fed at those altar rails; how many of the faithful departed that bell has rung to their rest; all the unwritten stories that are commemorated in these stones."*[114]

On the sanctuary were 18 other priests including the parish priests of 7 daughter parishes, Fr. Szymankiewicz of the Polish parish, Fr. Hudson, chaplain to the Little Sisters of the Poor and the Abbot of Downside who assisted Bishop Brunner. In the pews were relatives of the architect of St. Marie's, Mrs and Miss Hadfield (formerly of Sheffield), the Lord Mayor and Lady Mayoress of Sheffield (Alderman Keeble Hawson and his wife) and the leader of the City Council, Alderman J.H. Bingham.

After the Mass, a celebration luncheon was held at the Royal Victoria Station Hotel.

Monsignor Ronald Knox with Bishop Brunner and the Lord Mayor and Lady Mayoress of Sheffield after the Centenary Mass

Later that month, on Thursday 28th September, the junior children of St. Marie's School presented, to a full house at the City Hall, a Pageant and Tableaux to celebrate the centenary. The souvenir programme[115] shows the opening tableau was the peeling of hand-bells by children representing the eight bells of St. Marie's, together with a narrator, and a child dressed as an angel representing the Angelus bell. Then came a presentation featuring children in the roles, among others, of Fr. Pratt, Mr Hadfield the architect and Benjamin Gregory, the foreman builder. Children in the next presentation represented the religious and secular teachers of the parish's Catholic schools, one child each representing the sisters of Notre Dame, the Sisters of Charity, the Sisters of Mercy, the Little Sisters of the Poor, a Sister of the Poor Child Jesus, a Carmelite, a De La Salle brother and a lay teacher. Another aspect of St. Marie's history followed, featuring major benefactors to St. Marie's including the Duke of Norfolk. This was followed by a pageant with eleven children representing eleven Sheffield parishes. The next scene represented a verbal exchange between a child representing Catholic Action and another representing the Devil. The finale was of nine children representing children of the world of different nationalities, indicating the universality of the Church.

113   *Sheffield Telegraph.*
114   *St Marie's Catholic Monthly*, cited in Mgr. S. Sullivan's *A Short History of St. Marie's* and included in *St. Marie's Cathedral History and Guide* (1988).
115   I am grateful to Mrs Eileen Maher (née Loomes), who took part in this celebration, for this programme.

The front cover and the programme of the Centenary Pageant and Tableaux and the inside pages showing the names of the children from St. Marie's who took part

The Presentation of
The Centenary History of
St. Marie's

IN

PAGEANT and TABLEAUX

BY THE

JUNIOR CHILDREN OF ST. MARIE'S SCHOOL,

THURSDAY, SEPTEMBER 28th,
— 1950 —

To Celebrate the Centenary of St. Marie's Church.

✠

Souvenir Programme.

1850 ◆◆◆◆◆◆◆◆◆ A.M.D.G. ◆◆◆◆◆◆◆◆◆

Builder Good

1. Prologue ... ... St. Marie's Centenary

2. St. Marie's Bells appear in Pageant ... ...
   The Spirit of the Bells, introducing the Angelus
   Bell and the Clarion of Eight Bells
   Junior 1.

3. The Founder of the Church ... ...
   Junior 3 and 4 Boys.

4. The Teachers of the Schools ... ...
   Junior 4 Girls.

5. Ringing in of the Centenary of the Hierarchy ...
   Junior 3, Boys and Girls.

6. The Parishes ... ...
   Junior 2, Boys and Girls.

7. Present Activities ... ...
   Junior 3 and 4, Girls.

8. Ringing in of the Holy Year ... ...
   Junior 1, Boys and Girls.

9. Epilogue ... ... St. Marie's Centenary

1.

Centenary	Peter Kenrick
Angel of St. Marie's...	Annette Milner
Angelus Bell... ...	Veronica Street

Peal of Bells—
Deidre Milner, June Dawson, Anne
Nevin, Theresa Grayson, Monica
Toole, Veronica Snaith, Anne Hope,
June Brackenborough

Election Team

2.

Narrator ...	...Horace Kenworthy	Father Kavanagh ...	Vincent Askew
Father Pratt ...	Ralph Dickins	Mr. Hadfield ...	Geoffrey Leach
Missioner ...	Michael Parker	Benjamin Gregory ...	Roger Middleton *Good*

3—Teachers.

Sister of Notre Dame ...	Mary Davison	Carmelite ...	... Anne Ibbotson
Sister of Charity ...	Pauline Ford	Sister of Poor Child Jesus	
Little Sister of the Poor			Patricia Oldfield
	Maxine Cannetti	De La Salle Brother ...	Brian Thorneloe
Sister of Mercy ...	Catherine Headford	Secular Teacher ...	Pauline Hepworth

4—Spirits of Benefactors.

Bishop Knight ...	Michael Dempsey	Cardinal Wiseman	... Walter Glover
Duke of Norfolk ...	... Geoffrey Tate	Canon Dolan	David Leslie

5—The Parishes.

Elaine Pinchbeck	Angela Moxon	Gerald Boulding
Eileen Loomes	Pauline Higgins	Keith Williamson
Molly Whelan	Roy Bennett	Robert Dickins
Eileen Milner	Michael Peet	

6.

Catholic Action ...	Wendy Synnott	Devil	Dorothy Knowles
		Devils	

7—Children of the World.

U.S.A.	...Josephine Brammer	Yellow	...Joseph Curtain
Britain	Theresa Marcon	Wales	... Ann West
China	Graham Darling	Ireland	Maureen Clarke
Black	... Paul Costello	Scotland	Maureen Crowley
Red	...Douglas Leslie		

◆◆◆◆◆◆◆◆◆ **1950** ◆◆◆◆◆◆◆◆◆

A New Parish Priest

In March 1951, John Carmel Heenan was consecrated at Leeds as the successor to Bishop Poskitt. Bishop Heenan was *"a man of great charm, a gifted speaker and had fresh and enthusiastic ideas. He was convinced that the advantages in a priest staying many years in a parish were outweighed by the new opportunities and freshness that can come to both priest and people by a change"*.[116] Within months St. Marie's experienced the full effect of this viewpoint. Three of the curates, Frs. Michael O'Sullivan, Nicholas Kennedy and Bernard Jackson were moved and replaced.

Canon Collins on pilgrimage to Lourdes. Also in the photo is Fr. Horrax, a former parishioner of St. Marie's

John Carmel Heenan when Bishop of Leeds

On 15th June Canon Bradley, who had served as Parish Priest for sixteen years, was moved from St. Marie's to take up duties as the Administrator of St. Ann's Cathedral in Leeds. *St. Marie's Catholic Monthly* reports that Canon Bradley had been regarded by fellow members of the Sheffield Education Committee as *"an asset in all their deliberations and that his opinions were listened to with careful attention"*. One member of the committee had remarked that with Canon Bradley *"the defence of Catholic Schools and of Catholic Education is in capable hands"*. Within the Catholic sector, Canon Bradley had been, for many years, the Chief Diocesan Inspector of Schools and had also been, for several years, on the Diocesan Schools Commission. But it was at St. Marie's, the parish magazine records, that *"his life was centred – the place of prayer and instruction and inspiring ceremonial, all of which were carried out with great care and attention. It is by these things most of all that we would hope to remember him"*.

That same day, Canon Bradley's successor came to St. Marie's from St. Anne's Cathedral. Effectively the two priests had swapped roles in that the Cathedral Administrator now took up the role of Parish Priest of St. Marie's. Monsignor Canon John Dinn was born in Bradford, and his early education towards priesthood was at St. Bede's College in Bradford and then at St. Joseph's College at Mount Melleray near Waterford. From there he was chosen to continue his studies at the English College in Rome and was awarded a doctorate in philosophy and theology by the Gregorian University.

Monsignor John Dinn

116   Sullivan *A Short History of St. Marie's* p 26.

It is not recorded how either priest felt about the switching of roles, but since Monsignor Dinn was also Vicar General for the diocese, his arrival at St. Marie's could have been seen as increasing the status of St. Marie's to the second church of the diocese after the cathedral.

Memories of Childhood at St. Marie's

Eileen Maher (née Loomes) remembers the occasion at St. Marie's school[117] when Monsignor Dinn, the new Parish Priest, was formally welcomed to the school at the annual prize giving. The occasion was special since, before he gave out the prize certificates, Monsignor Dinn was presented with his robes as a Domestic Prelate. Canon White, from Leeds, was standing in for Bishop Heenan for the occasion. Following the prize giving, the very popular hymn "Faith of our Fathers" was sung for all to join in. Finally there was the presentation of the Scouts' Flag to St. Marie's troop and the singing of the National Anthem.

The front cover and inside pages of the souvenir programme for the school prizegiving and the presentation of his robes as a domestic prelate to Monsignor Dinn

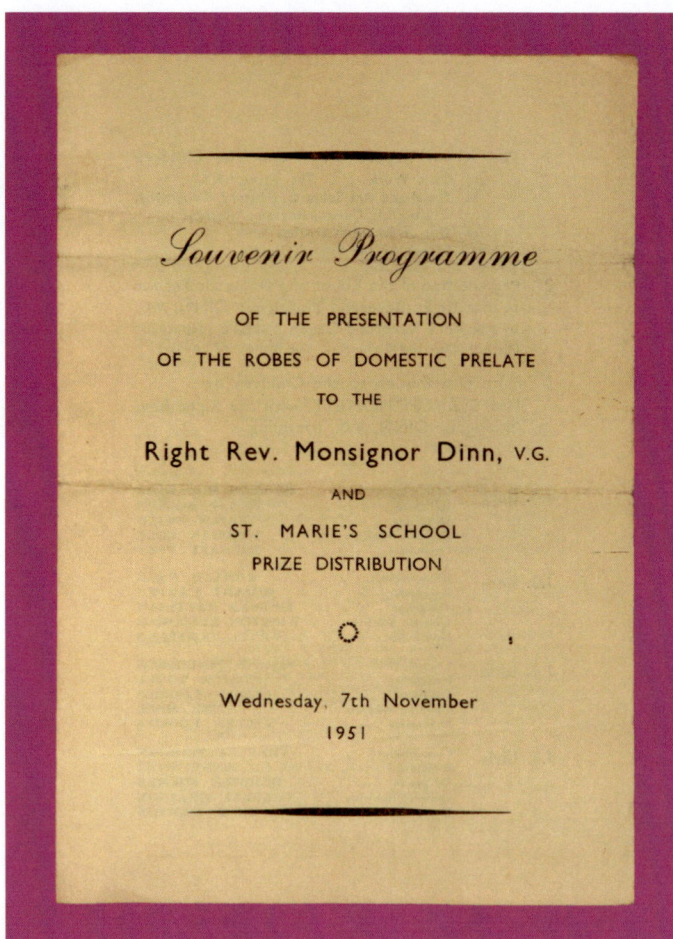

Souvenir Programme

OF THE PRESENTATION
OF THE ROBES OF DOMESTIC PRELATE
TO THE

Right Rev. Monsignor Dinn, V.G.

AND

ST. MARIE'S SCHOOL
PRIZE DISTRIBUTION

Wednesday, 7th November
1951

1. The School Report . . The Children
   (a) Basic Work . . The Three "R's"
   (b) Social and Art Subjects (History, Geography, Crafts, P.T. Games, Rhythm, Singing).
   (c) Out of School Activities.
   (d) Speech by the School Captain.

2. Presentation of the Robes of a Domestic Prelate to the Right Reverend Monsignor DINN, V.G. by the Very Reverend Canon WHITE (deputy for His Lordship the Right Rev. the Bishop of Leeds).

3. Prize Distribution to the Children by Mrs. STANLEY MOFFETT, with the Right Rev. Monsignor DINN, V.G., presiding.

J.4. Boys		
Class-Subject . .	GERALD BOULDING
Religious . . .	PHILIP HOBSON
Diligence . . .	BRIAN SMITH
General Subjects . .	NORMAN COLE
Dramatics . . .	MICHAEL PEET

J.3. Boys		
Class-Subject . . .	RONALD CARR
Religious	ROBERT CARTER
Diligence . . .	THOMAS RATTIGAN
General Subjects . .	WINSTON LUSCOMBE
Dramatics . . .	PAUL COSTELLO

J.4. Girls		
Class-Subject . .	ELAINE PINCHBECK
Religious . . .	MONICA TOOLE
Diligence . . .	EILEEN LOOMES
General Subjects . .	ANNE HOPE
Dramatics . . .	EILEEN LOOMES

J.3. Girls		
Class-Subject . .	THERESA MARCON
Religious . . .	ANNE WEST
Diligence . . .	DEIRDRE MILNER
General Subjects .	THERESA GRAYSON
Dramatics . . .	JUNE DAWSON

Junior II.		
Class-Subject . .	ANNE KAYE and RICHARD VAZ
Religious	DAVID AWDAS
Diligence . .	ROSEMARY BOOKER
General Subjects . .	JANET CROSS
Dramatics . .	ANTHONY CHARLESWORTH

Junior I.		
Class-Subject . .	JAMES CONNORTON
Religious .	BERNADETTE McGOWAN
Diligence . .	BARRY SMITH
General Subjects . .	ANNE REYNOLDS
Dramatics . .	MICHAEL DRIVER

Infants 2nd year		
Class-Subject . . .	PETER DODD
Religious . .	BERNARD GRIERSON
Diligence . .	EILEEN WYLIE
General Subjects . .	VICTORIA MEEKE

Infants 1st year		
Class-Subject . .	CHRISTINE DARLING
Religious	LINDA CARR
Diligence . .	FRANCISCA POMERANSKI
General Subjects . .	MARIE WOULFE

Reception Class		
Class-Subject . . .	RONALD ENOCH
Religious . .	JACQUELINE NEVIN
Diligence . .	KRISTINA MAYNARD
General Subjects . .	ANNE MALONE
Art	PAULINE HOBSON VINCENT ASKEW
Dramatics . .	MICHAEL DEMPSEY MAXINE CANNETTI
Sports . .	MAUREEN HOLLIDAY ANTHONY GILLOTT

Scholarship Results, 1951 WILLIAM WOOD, ROGER MIDDLETON BRIAN THORNELOE, PATRICK MALLOY MICHAEL MOORHOUSE, ANTHONY CARL ANNE IBBOTSON, VERONICA STREET PAULINE HEPWORTH, PAULINE HIGGINS DOROTHY KNOWLES, PAULINE SCRIMSHAW

4. "Faith of Our Fathers" (Please join in)

5. Presentation of the Scouts' Flag—
   St. Maries' Troop

6. God Save the King.

Living memory, of course, goes back further. Pat Holmes, now retired to Newark, remembers many of the children at St. Marie's school from 1944 to 1948. They were Dawn Burton, Joyce Wilson, Norma Woodhead, Dorothy Leslie, Hazel Leach, Betty and Dorothy Woodall, Maureen Ewington, Monica Axelby, Hun Sherry, Pat, Marie and Monica O'Toole, Annie Sergent, Catherine and Rae Canetti, Valerie Leach, Betty Pickering, Julie Hirst, Paddy Latham, Mavis Pilkington, Sheila Eason, Kathleen Grant, the twins Dorothy and Maureen Conorton, Pat Oldfield, Janice Oats, Peter Millington, Sean and Fergus McClary, Billy Lunscolm and Anthony Selex. Teachers remembered were Miss O'Brien, Miss Josey Smith, Mrs White, Miss Worth and the Sisters of Notre Dame, Sr. Mary and the stern head teacher, Sr. Hilary.

Tony Danaher, now living in Canada, recalls many people active in St. Marie's in the post-war years. From 1947 and beyond he remembers the organist Edward Hirst and *'fine gentlemen and good singers'* from the choir, Sam Wolfe, Henry Malloy, Bill Driver and Bill Whelan. The altar servers included Peter Mullins, Joe Tyrell, Wilf Doyle, Mark Hodges, Pat Danaher and George and Bill

Wood. For many years the sacristan was George Evinson who is recalled as being very strict with the sacristy very much in his charge. Harry Hurst was the chief bell ringer. It was he who assembled the team that rang the bells on various occasions and, every Sunday, the Angelus bell. For the centennial celebrations, Harry restored the sanctuary lamp which was suspended over the sanctuary.

And there were always characters around. *"I recall old Miss Jones who hailed from the Burngreave area of the city, who went to early Mass at St. Catherine's and then off to St. Vincent's and finally just making it to St. Marie's where she always sat in the front"*. *"Old Joe Taffe"* was another character always at Sunday Mass, as was Hubert Callaghan *"who always got to Mass late and made a noise walking to the front of the church in his studded boots, complaining that Mass always started too early for him to get there on time"*. Not least, Tony recalls the *"wonderful priests"*, Canon Bradley assisted by Fr. Kennedy, Fr. Jackson and Fr. O'Sullivan, later to be joined by a Polish priest. *"Every Sunday they had their Mass that ended with them singing their National Anthem with great pride"*.

The crowning of Our Lady's statue by the May Queen in 1960 showing Mgr. Dinn, Fr. Peter McGuire (to his right),
Fr. John Murphy (to his left and as a deacon) and Fr. Michael Szymankiewicz at the rear.

The annual May processions were important in parish life and in the lives of young girls in particular. Eileen Maher remembers fondly the May procession of 1952 when she was chosen to be May Queen. With celebrations both at St. Marie's school and in church, the crowning of the statue of Our Lady in church had moved, over the years, from the upstairs Munster chapel to the front of the sanctuary. Always a special occasion, the greatest honour was to be the child who, as May Queen, placed the crown on the statue during the afternoon devotion.

Similarly important in the childhood memories was the annual procession of the Blessed Sacrament on or around the feast day of Corpus Christi each June. The gardens and lawns of St. Elizabeth's Home at Heeley were the setting for this open air event, when children who had received their first Holy Communion took a central role. In later years the venue for the annual procession moved from St. Elizabeth's home to the grounds of the Notre Dame convent at Oakbrook and continued until the mid 1970s.

As an example of active parish service, Mary Hirst remembers St. Anne's House, just off Weston Bank

The 1952 May Queen and attendants, with cushion bearer Mary West and her helpers

behind the Spiritualist church. She recalls her mother visiting and providing practical help for single retired women at this small home run by the Catholic Women's League. It was a converted house with bedsits and was later expanded by the purchase of the house next door. A live-in couple were employed there. Few people remember this small but valued project.

The 1952 May Queen and attendants. Left to right: Eileen Pinchbeck, Anne Hope, Eileen Loomes (May Queen), Monica Toole, Eileen Milner. Photo taken in one of the school classrooms.

The 1950 Corpus Christi procession passing outbuildings at St. Elizabeth's Home.
Photograph taken from an upper floor window.

The 1959 wedding of Denis Evinson and Hazel Leach. Fr. Peter McGuire celebrated the Nuptial Mass

Mary Hirst remembers, too, her sister, Julia, leaving the family and the parishioners of St. Marie's to enter the Carmelite convent at Kirkedge where she took the name Sister Mary of the Assumption.[118]

Edward Hurst shares a farewell embrace with his daughter Julia after Mass and moments before she entered the nuns' enclosure at Kirkedge.
Julia is dressed as a bride and was accompanied by some fifty well-wishers from her family and parish

Housing and Population Changes

The 1950s saw the later stages of slum clearance and the expansion of Sheffield's huge re-housing programme. Even into the 1950s, appalling living conditions continued in many inner city pockets. The Duke Street area in particular was seriously overcrowded, with slum dwelling continuing to deteriorate. It was from these conditions that parishioners Cyril and Justine Morewood were re-housed to Norfolk Park. Parishioners who had lived in the areas above the Ponds Forge furnaces tell of how each morning, soot would belch from the furnace chimneys and fall onto any clean washing inadvertently left out on washing lines. The air was poor and buildings everywhere were blackened with decades of soot and dirt. Paul Helliwell, as a child in the 1950s and early sixties, and later through his involvement in the SVP, remembers a "doss house" in Townhead Street. The SVP gave out tokens to enable destitute men to get a bed there for the night. He recalls, too, the special coins the SVP gave to poor families that were exchangeable for groceries in a shop in Duke Street run by a Catholic family. *"I don't think people realize today how poverty-stricken this area was"*[119]. Angela Pritchard, a parishioner as a child, remembers her mother taking her to St. Marie's school, sometimes in dense smog. It was the frequency of smog and the general bad air in Sheffield

that caused her father, who had a chest condition, to move the family out of Sheffield, in 1954, to live in Grantham. On into the early 1960s *"the city centre was pretty grim. There were still bombed out buildings, war-damaged and never replaced"*[120].

During the 1960s, at last, new housing was being built close to the city centre even on the same site as previous slum dwelling, as with the large Park Hill flats complex near Duke Street. Further out of town where the air was cleaner, major housing estates were built, for example, out at Gleadless Valley, Batemoor, Jordansthorpe and Greenhill. One effect of this continuing move of people away from the city centre was the falling number of parishioners within the parish boundaries of St. Marie's and the continuing corresponding need for suburban churches.

Already before the 1939-45 war St. Marie's had supported the building of parishes at the Manor, Arbourthorne and Wybourn estates. Now a chapel of ease was opened to serve the new housing being built at Lodge Moor, even further out than Fulwood and Crosspool from where a few former parishioners remember, as children, walking the long road to St. Marie's for Sunday Mass. In 1957, a redundant school room and former library at Benty Lane was acquired to serve as a chapel. Supplied from St. Marie's until 1968, this hall went on to serve as the church for the new daughter parish of St. Francis[121].

A photograph taken in 1960 by the City Engineer to show the conditions in homes due to be demolished

---

118   After many years as a professed nun, Sister Mary volunteered to go to Slovenia to help form a new monastery seeking the same Carmelite discipline as Kirkedge. When it transpired that more nuns were required to sustain the new foundation, Sister Mary chose to stay in the new monastery with Sister Raphael who had travelled with her to Slovenia from Kirkedge. In 2016 she was still living there as an enclosed nun.

119   Interviewed by the author in September 2017.

120   Ibid.

121   This arrangement continued for more than 30 years, until land was donated by Miss Marian Young of The Croft next to the present church was built in 1989.

The 1950s and 60s, too, saw the beginnings of significant immigration into Sheffield, though at a smaller scale than in many other large cities. Perhaps because of the slowing down of production in the steelworks after the war, and perhaps also because the nature of Sheffield's main industries did not need high numbers of new and unskilled workers, the number of people arriving to settle in Sheffield was not large. The 1951 Census for Sheffield records a total population of 577,000 but with only 2,535 residents who were born in Ireland; 1,206 born in Poland, 665 born in Germany, 587 born in India, 78 born in Pakistan and 32 born in Jamaica. But the provisions of the 1948 British Nationality Act were only beginning to take effect. Under this Act, any Commonwealth citizen could claim British citizenship and residency in UK as their mother country. This 'open door' policy was to attract much needed labour into this country particularly for building work, for labour intensive manufacturing industries and to work on buses and trains.

Among the first nationalities who took up this free entry were workers from Jamaica. The reception they experienced in Sheffield (as elsewhere) was often unwelcoming. In 1956 and again in 1958, *The Star* reported that Mr Bingham, of Sheffield Council's Department of Social Services, wrote to the Secretary of State asking for a Welfare Officer to be sent from the Colonial Office in Whitehall to help with inter-racial community work. Tensions were running high as graffiti appeared calling to 'keep Britain white'. Accusations were made through newspapers that Commonwealth workers were 'taking jobs by accepting lower wages'. Interviews conducted by *The Star* at Kelvin Caribbean Lunch Club recorded maltreatment in public places and very poor housing; "*I lived in Brunswick St., Broomhall. It was terrible. The digs were shocking, indescribable. It didn't matter how big your family was, you had to live in one room. It was cold and damp – we ended up in the worst housing. It's terrible what we leave behind – my home in Barbados was lovely...*"[122]

Years later (and before the restrictions brought in through the 1962 Commonwealth Immigrants Act), *The Star* was able to report (in the language and style of the time) "*Hundreds of coloured folk have settled down (in Attercliffe) and built good relations and friendships with white people, and white people have befriended the coloureds*".

Parishioner Mavis Hamilton recalls arriving from Jamaica alone, aged 20, to live with a cousin already in Sheffield. She recalls arriving late on a March evening. It was dark but she could see and smell the smoke rising from what she thought were hundreds of factories. It was only next morning that she realized that what she had seen were just the houses, each one with smoke billowing out. The tall factory chimneys were giving out much more smoke.

Mavis Hamilton on the first Holy Communion Day of her daughter, Beverley

Mavis found work, through her cousin, in a cutlery factory. Though she experienced some anti-Black racist remarks (especially after a long-term friend arrived from Jamaica and the couple married), life at St. Marie's, Mavis recalled, was trouble-free. She was the only black face in the congregation. Whilst services felt very sombre, Mavis enjoyed especially the Summer parish trips to the seaside and dancing at Top Rank or at parish dances in the Notre Dame school hall on Fulwood Road.

Soon, meetings exploring the Catholic faith began in the newly opened room under the sacristies. With four small children, one of whom died tragically, and living as a lone parent, Mavis says, "*The Church became my life. The Church saved me*". It was Mavis who helped start a Sunday school for children, though sometimes only her three came along. It was only in much later years that a children's liturgy was introduced into the Sunday Mass.

---

122   Cited in *The 1950s*, a Sheffield Local Studies Library PowerPoint presentation for schools (325.1.5). Also recorded there is the story of an Attercliffe bar manager who deliberately broke glasses and then called the police to move the black customers on.

Chapter VIII
Development, Change and Renewal 1960 -1980

The two decades leading up to 1980 were times of considerable change at St. Marie's, in the city and in society. The drab, post-war years of austerity slowly gave way to the beginnings of a more colourful, daring and 'liberated' society where luxuries like television, fridges and even cars became possibilities for many households. By July 1957, the Prime Minister could claim, "*Indeed, let us be frank about it – most of our people have never had it so good*"[123]. Whilst prosperity was beginning to rise, many in Sheffield and other northern cities still lived in harsh conditions and were not experiencing the consumerism beginning to expand elsewhere. Cinemas and Dance Halls, still very popular entertainments, began declining as home television sales expanded. Within the Catholic community, too, change was considerable, especially in the 1960s and 1970s during and following the Second Vatican Council.

Developments involving Schools

Following the wartime destruction of St. Marie's school in Sheaf Gardens, the girls from there moved in with the boys at the Edmund Road site. The girls' school occupied the downstairs whilst the boys confined themselves to the upstairs. Overcrowding was resolved in 1944 when St. Marie's became a single primary school taking both boys and girls but only until aged 11. From that age, pupils now moved on to secondary education either at De La Salle College, Osgathorpe (boys) or Notre Dame High School Fulwood (girls).

The 1960s saw considerable government money provided for new schools. New Catholic secondary schools were built in 1959 (St. Peter's at Parson Cross), in 1962 (St. Paul's on 16 acres of Norfolk family land in Granville Road) and in 1965 (St. John Fisher at Handsworth). These schools catered for those who had not passed the new 11-plus examinations and, thus, could not go to the Grammar schools at De La Salle or Notre Dame.

By 1968, the aging 1878 St. Marie's school in Edmund Road needed replacing.

A site for a new school was found on the edge of Norfolk Park overlooking the city but, by 1970, a change of plan sited the new school in the grounds of the Notre Dame convent on Fulwood Road. Built to a modern specification for the changed needs of teaching, the new St. Marie's Primary School included a hall and kitchens capable of serving 320 lunchtime meals to pupils. The school was now to occupy its fourth building since its foundation in 1833.

St. Marie's School in Edmund Road

It was planned that the old Edmund Road school building might be converted into a Catholic youth club on the ground floor and into a hostel for homeless men on the upper floor. But objections from local residents dampened the hope for the hostel and, within a year, vandals had set fire to the empty building. The damage from this made demolition a necessity. But the idea of a hostel went ahead and a property closer to the city centre in Hanover Street was bought. "Bethlehem House", as it

---

123   Harold Macmillan's speech to Conservative Party at Bedford.

was named, was run for its first few years by volunteer parishioners of St. Marie's, before later being taken into the professional sector.

Further changes involving the Catholic secondary schools to which young people of the parish could go came in 1977. All Saints comprehensive school was formed. This was achieved by expanding the capacity of the buildings at St. Paul's school (and including 6th form provision) and amalgamating this school with the De La Salle College which was then phased out by ceasing to take new pupils.

Canon George Collins

The original St. Marie's school in Surrey Street, built in 1823. Photo taken after 1890 when the Town Hall, in the background, was built. After Edmund Road school had opened, this building became a registry office.

Changes to the Clergy

In September 1964, after more than 12 years as Parish Priest at St. Marie's, Monsignor John Dinn died. His obituary in the 1965 Leeds Diocese Directory speaks of his setting an example for other priests in his pastoral zeal and by his courteous, refined manner, "*Many sought his advice and guidance which he gave so generously… the diocese mourns the passing of a very great priest*". Archbishop Heenan interrupted his attendance at the Second Vatican Council to conduct the funeral. The obituary continues, "*the tremendous congregation of clergy, civic dignitaries and people was evidence enough of the great esteem and affection in which he was held*".

Canon Collins in 1966 at the raising of a new cross for the East gable end. The former one, described by Cecil Higgins in 1940 as loose, fell down in 1962

Mgr. Dinn's replacement at St. Marie's was Fr. George Collins, a very different man, born in Rotherham in 1910 and educated at Ushaw. Already working in Sheffield, as Parish Priest at St. Patrick's, Lane Top, Fr. Collins was moved to St. Marie's at the death of Mgr. Dinn, later becoming a Canon of the Diocese.

In 1966 the East gable-end cross was finally replaced. It had blown down four years earlier from the unstable mounting discovered by Cecil Higgins in 1940. Though quiet and unassuming, George Collins showed himself to be loyal and attentive to what was needed.

Canon Collins served at St. Marie's for less than four years, until another appointment took him elsewhere in the diocese. He returned to Sheffield twelve years later, when ill health overcame him. He was received into the care of the Sisters of Mercy at Claremont Hospital where he later died. Canon Collins' obituary in the Diocesan Directory records that *"he died on the feast of the Annunciation, 25th March 1980. [He] always had a great devotion to Our Lady and was a regular member of the Diocesan Pilgrimage to Lourdes."*

But the biggest change to the clergy operating from St. Marie's in the 1960s was, of course, the appointment by Bishop Wheeler of Mgr. Gerald Moverley to be an auxiliary bishop for the Leeds diocese based at St. Marie's.

Gerald Moverley was born in Bradford in 1922. His family could be traced back to pre-Reformation days and had remained Catholic right though the penal centuries, living near Hazelwood and employed and protected by the wealthy Catholic Vavascour family. After grammar schooling at St. Bede's, Bradford, he trained for the priesthood at Ushaw College, being ordained priest in 1946. After a very short spell in a parish, Fr. Moverley was called to Bishop's House to work as Bishop Poskitt's secretary. Within three years, the bishop fell sick with an illness that was both prolonged and terminal. The 27 year old Fr. Moverley found himself with more and more responsibilities, a situation that continued well beyond Bishop Poskitt's death in 1950 because of the long delay in appointing a new bishop.

Bishop Heenan, soon after his appointment to Leeds, offered Fr. Moverley a complete change and he went to study in Rome for a Doctorate in Canon Law, which he completed in 1954. He returned home to set up an improved Diocesan Curia and Tribunal. He was also appointed, again, as secretary to the bishop. In 1956 he became Canon Moverley, continuing to work at Leeds Cathedral, becoming both the Chancellor of the diocese and a founder member of the Canon Law Society. In 1957 Bishop Heenan was translated to Liverpool to be archbishop there, Bishop George Patrick Dwyer was consecrated as Bishop of Leeds and Canon Moverley finally became a parish priest.

When, in 1965, Bishop Dwyer was translated to Birmingham to become archbishop there, Bishop William Gordon Wheeler was appointed Bishop of Leeds. Soon after his appointment, he petitioned Rome for an auxiliary bishop to help him with so large a diocese. In December 1967 the news arrived that Pope Paul VI, who had made Canon Moverley a monsignor just two years earlier, had granted the petition and chosen Mgr. Moverley as the first auxiliary bishop of Leeds. The new bishop was to assist by having pastoral responsibility for the parishes of the southern part of the Leeds diocese and was to operate from St. Marie's church in Sheffield.

The Consecration of Bishop Moverley

Bishop Gerald Moverley

On 25th January 1968 St. Marie's was the setting for the ordination of Gerald Moverley as a bishop. The three consecrating bishops were the Right Reverend William Gordon Wheeler, Bishop of Leeds (the principal consecrator), the Most Reverend George Dwyer, Archbishop of Birmingham, and the Right Reverend John McClean, Bishop of Middlesbrough. Also taking part was Archbishop Heenan, by now both Archbishop of Westminster and a Cardinal. He preached at the Mass. Bishop Moverley's brother, Fr. Charles Moverley was present as was the Parish Priest of St. Marie's, Canon Collins. Among the many clergy guests was the Abbot of Ampleforth, the Rt. Rev. Basil Hume, later to become Cardinal Hume.

Bishop Moverley lies prostrate
at the concluding prayer of the litany of the saints
during his ordination as a bishop

Cardinal Heenan presides as the three consecrating bishops lay their hands on Bishop Moverley
Canon Collins is seated next to the Cardinal

The notes provided for the press before the ceremony give detail of timings. *"Cardinal Heenan is expected to arrive at St. Marie's presbytery at 10.15am. The Clergy Procession will enter the church at 10.30am. The Civic Processions will enter the church at 10.45am. The procession of visiting Church Dignitaries will enter the church at 10.50am and will be followed by the procession of the Consecrating Bishops, Bishop Moverley and the other Ministers of the Ceremony. It is expected that the Ceremony will last between one and a half and two hours"*

During the Mass, interestingly, a priest was there to lead the congregation in their participation in the Mass including the Gloria and the Creed in English. This was Fr. Stephen Sullivan. After the anointing of the new bishop with oil, the crozier presented to Bishop Moverley as a sign of his pastoral office was the brass one used by Bishop Cornthwaite as Bishop of Beverley which bore his crest in enamel. Alongside this link to the past, a new feature of this post-Vatican II ordination Mass was that the three consecrating bishops concelebrated Mass together with the new bishop.

This mixture of old and new reflected the choice of motto that Bishop Moverley incorporated into his episcopal coat of arms. The Latin words *"nova et vetera"* allude to a line in Matthew's Gospel (Matt 13: 46) *"Every scribe who becomes a disciple of the kingdom of heaven is like a householder who brings out from his storeroom things both new and old"*. The design of the crest shows the white rose of Yorkshire and a sword to represent Sheffield, the "steel city".

As an auxiliary bishop, Bishop Moverley did not have an episcopal see. Following a custom of the Church, the new bishop was assigned the name of an ancient see no longer active. Bishop Moverley's titular see was to be Tinisa, a bishopric in part of what is now Tunisia, which fell into disuse after the Islamic invasions of North Africa in the seventh and eighth centuries.

Following Bishop Moverley's Ordination Mass a Reception was held in the recently built Top Rank Suite in Arundel Gate. The notes for the press record that *"After the Loyal Toast, the Archbishop of Birmingham will propose a toast of "The New Bishop". Bishop Moverley will then reply. Bishop Wheeler will then propose the toast "Our Guests" and the Lord Mayor of Sheffield will reply"*

Shortly after his ordination as bishop, Gerald Moverley visited Rome and met Pope Paul VI. The new bishop chose Canon Collins to accompany him on this visit, perhaps aware that he would soon be moved away from St. Marie's.

Bishop Moverley and Canon Collins in Rome with Pope Paul VI in 1968

Another New Parish Priest

Bishop Moverley was, until 1980, auxiliary bishop of Leeds Diocese. He was not Parish Priest of St. Marie's nor was St. Marie's a cathedral. St. Marie's remained a parish of the Leeds Diocese with its own Parish Priest. It was just one of 50 parishes served and shepherded by the new auxiliary bishop.

Soon after the ordination to episcopacy of Bishop Moverley, Canon Collins was moved by Bishop Wheeler from St. Marie's to a Harrogate parish. Two months later, Father Stephen Sullivan was appointed new Parish Priest[124].

Monsignor Sullivan, as he is remembered, served as Parish Priest at St. Marie's for 17 years. In those days The Rectory[125] always had a number of curates which Mgr. Sullivan gently tried to nurture in ministry, even those who were more headstrong or prone to playing pranks on him. Paul Helliwell, a lifelong parishioner, remembers playing football at the rear of St. Marie's, with other altar boys or sometimes with one of the curates. Outside the sacristy corridor was a grassed area taking half the area now used as a car park. This grassy flat area was several feet above the small area behind the priests' house where a car might be parked. This grassed level was the last remnant of the area, which, before St. Marie's was built, was set aside for Catholic burials[126].

Mgr. Sullivan is warmly remembered. His obituary in the Leeds Diocese Yearbook records, *"Despite his many commitments he always remained a warm and kindly priest, anxious at all times to help anyone who sought his assistance"*. This is borne out by the memories of parishioners from his days as Parish Priest in the

124   Fr. Sullivan became a Domestic Prelate, with the honourary title of Monsignor in 1971.
125   As the priest's house, now named Cathedral House, was known.
126   The area is now fully levelled as a car park.

Monsignor Stephen Sullivan

and, thereby, better to reach out to the needs and hopes of the world. Perhaps the first changes arising from Vatican II that became apparent in every local church were in the way Catholics celebrated the Eucharist (Mass).

Paul Helliwell remembers serving Mass before the changes from Vatican II were introduced. He would often be late for school because he was the server at the 8am weekday Mass. He recalls the Latin prayers and the Latin responses he made on behalf of the congregation, the many signs of the cross throughout the Mass and the strict rules to be followed in smallest detail. Every word, even the readings from Scripture, was in Latin. For the weekday Masses, he and the priest would be at the altar in St. Joseph Chapel and the congregation was silent and some distance away in the North aisle pews. Kneeling behind the priest he observed once or twice, maybe on occasions when the priest had arrived in the sacristy just in time for Mass, not black trousers but the stripes of pyjamas.

Changes in the celebration of Mass gradually appeared through the 1960s, beginning with the scripture readings being in English and the steadily increasing involvement of all present in the words and actions of worship. One aim of the changes to the liturgy was to encourage "full, conscious and active participation" by all present in the prayer of the Mass[127]. This was very evident in the role undertaken by Fr. Sullivan, as he then was, in leading the people in their responses at the Ordination Mass of Bishop Moverley in 1968.

One of the very visible changes in Catholic churches following Vatican II was the introduction of altars at which the priest faced the people, symbolizing and encouraging active participation and the recognition of the role of the laity and priest together in the celebration of Mass.

At St. Marie's, the rood screen and the distance between the existing altar and the people detracted from the purpose of this change to the Mass. To celebrate Mass facing the people, a simple wooden altar was constructed and positioned, first, in front of the rood screen (where, on a single step up from the nave it would be difficult to see) and, then, between the 1921 High Altar and the rood screen (where it was obscured behind the screen dividing the people from the sanctuary.

But efforts to achieve the desired changes to the Mass continued. A year after Bishop Moverley's Ordination Mass, which itself had emphasized the involvement of everyone present, Mgr. Sullivan, in the parish newsletter[128],

late 1960s and throughout the 1970s. Peter Collet, a parishioner for many years, recalls what he simply calls *"his genuine holiness"* and the day he and Mgr. Sullivan were talking of sanctity. The Monsignor, he recalls, was keen to point out how *"he and I were like little boats on a lake at the foot of tall mountains. People who were holy"*, the Monsignor said to him, *" were like those who had scaled those lofty mountains. We are at a much lower place. He was humble but so kind"*. Fr. Peter McGuire, who was a curate under the Monsignor, recalls him as *"so kind"*, *"a delight"*, *"able to speak devotedly and with ease of flow about the Eucharist"* and simply as *"saintly"*.

Changes in Parish Life and Worship

In the Autumns of the four years 1962 – 1965, Catholic bishops from all over the world met in Rome in what is known as the Second Vatican Council. Much of the groundwork for the changes within the Church that came from what is now known familiarly as "Vatican II" had been going on for more than fifty years. The Council sought to renew the life of the Church, to refresh attitudes

---

127   The Vatican II document, *Sacrosanctum Concilium* paragraph 14 spells out the intention of the Council in changes to the Mass: "Mother Church earnestly desires that all the faithful should be led out to that full, conscious and active participation in liturgical celebrations".

128   3rd August 1969 courtesy of Sheffield Archives.

The temporary altar facing the congregation placed inside the sanctuary

describes the changing and varied celebration of Mass at St. Marie's. *"There has gradually evolved a pattern for the different Masses on Sunday. The early Mass at 6.30am is a quiet Mass without much ceremony. 8am is as it has always been, a prayerful Mass without music. The most popular morning Mass is the one at 9.30am. Here we have begun the Sung English liturgy, with simple tunes that I am sure are easy to follow. Judging by the size of the congregation, this could be a real moving experience if only the shy ones would join in the singing. The 11am Mass is the sung Latin Mass as usual and the evening Mass, the best attended, is a community Mass"*.

The sung Latin Mass on Sundays was no longer the old High Mass with its elaborate ritual including priests taking the parts of deacon and sub-deacon. Instead it was the same Mass as the others, with the scripture readings in English but the familiar Missa de Angelis plainsong music for the Kyrie, Gloria, Credo, Sanctus and Angus Dei. The choir might also sing motets in Latin. But within a year, the parish newsletter records a discussion at a parish meeting at which concern was expressed that steps should be taken to ensure that the singing of the ordinary parts in Latin should not be forgotten. The decision was that these ordinary parts (e.g. the Creed and the Holy, Holy) be sung in Latin monthly at those Sunday Masses that had music. A month later, the parish newsletter reports *"mixed comments on the singing of*

the ordinary parts of the Mass in Latin. But", wrote Mgr. Sullivan, *"it is too soon to make a judgement."*

At a broader level, the newsletters of 1970 record some other effects of Vatican II's direction towards more active participation in the life of the Church by the laity. The attempt to form a Parish Council of lay people alongside the clergy for decision making were continuing. Additionally, adult education in the faith was strengthened through the provision of the Education Centre in the previously unused room beneath the sacristies. Further changes came in the form of the new English rites for the celebration of Baptism (July 1970) and Marriage (November 1970). The newsletter for 5th July records that in the new rite of Baptism (*"preferably celebrated within Sunday Mass"*) there is *"greater involvement in the ceremony required of the parents of the child, the godparents and the people present"*. Mrs Celia White recalls that her wedding in 1966 to a (then) "non-Catholic" was the first at St Marie's where a full Nuptial Mass was allowed for a "mixed" marriage. Celia wanted to receive Holy Communion on her wedding day but not without her new husband. To avoid any risk of upset to members of the congregation unfamiliar with new permissions that could be granted in these circumstances, Canon Collins proposed that Celia might receive Holy Communion on her wedding day by attending the 6.30am Mass which Celia willingly did.

Traditional devotional practices continued. The crowning of the statue of Our Lady by the May Queen carried on as before. The annual Corpus Christi procession continued each June but (from about 1970) at Notre Dame Convent grounds and not at Heeley Convent and Home for the elderly. A little later, the devotional service known as "Forty Hours"[129] was provided. But new practices were taking root. The October newsletter announces a House Mass to be held at a parishioner's home in Fulwood Road on a Thursday evening. In the October, too, the parish joined in a national pilgrimage to Rome for the canonisation of 40 English and Welsh martyrs. The popular enthusiasm for these new saints was similar to the enthusiasm shown in the parish in 1929 at the canonization of Sts. John Fisher and Thomas More. These latter two, with the Norfolk ancestor martyr Philip Howard, had been commemorated in the fabric of St. Marie's with the stained glass window in the North aisle (in 1896). The names of the Forty Martyrs were to be inscribed as a frieze at the top of the nave walls in 1972.

Dating from this time, too, was the formation of the Over Sixties club of the parish and, later, the Activities Group which provided companionship, fund-raising activities

129 "Quarant Ore" developed in Italy during the 17th century and came to England during the period of Ultramontane enthusiasm in the 19th century. "Forty Hours" is a long period of continuous, mostly private, prayer and meditation in church lasting for 40 hours and with the Consecrated Host placed on the altar and made visible in a monstrance (a metal vessel with a circular glass centre to contain the Host.

and hospitality for all sorts of occasions. Leading lights in this included Mary Kartawick, Lillian Horsfield and Lynne Todd. The Activities Group continued right through and beyond the 1990s.

Also beginning in 1970 and still continuing (2018) was the Sheffield LIFE group providing support for women and practical alternatives to abortion as part of a major national pro-life organisation. Fr. Peter McGuire, Mrs Eileen Maher and a wide range of parishioners of St. Marie's and other parishes became major workers in this movement.

Fuelled by enthusiasm flowing from the refreshed mood sweeping through the Church following Vatican II, new ventures in outreach and in exploring one's own faith through catechesis developed during the 1970s. The parish was growing in confidence and community. The catechetical centre established in the room beneath the sacristies and the parish library were both well used, encouraged by the enthusiasm especially of Fr. Donal O'Leary and, later, Fr. Brendan McKeefry, young curates of the parish.

During the 1970s there were always a range of curates at St. Marie's engaged in the life of a busy parish. Ten curates served at St. Marie's during the decade: Frs. Peter Grant, John Roach, Donal O'Leary, Peter Ward, Kevin Kelly, John Grady, Brendan McKeefry, Colum Kelly, John Kinsella and Peter McGuire. Lots of tasks fell to the curates, including visiting families and the schools and acting as chaplains to the hospitals within the parish – the Royal Hospital in West Street (later to integrate with the Royal Infirmary at Upperthorpe to form Hallamshire Hospital), St. George's Hospital for the elderly, the Jessop Hospital for Women and Sheffield Children's Hospital. Fr. Peter McGuire remembers how busy life was when he was at St. Marie's as a young curate from 1977, *"The doorbell was always going. We were on the go all the time. Priestly life was good".*

The 1972 Re-ordering of St. Marie's

The changes to Catholic liturgy introduced through Vatican II, in particular the call for full, conscious and active participation by the congregation, rendered unhelpful the layout of the sanctuary of St. Marie's based, as it was, on the needs of medieval liturgy[130]. For example, the rood screen clearly separated the clergy and the action of the Mass from the people. Additionally, the High Altar could not be used for celebrating Mass with the priest facing the people. Early in 1972, Mgr. Sullivan was able to announce in the parish newsletter, *"After a three year period of thorough consultation and experimentation on the re-ordering of our beautiful Gothic church for the*

celebration of the new liturgy, Mr Frame of J.J. Frame was consulted to give us his ideas....A particular care [was]...to ensure that any new material introduced is linked in some way with features already present [in the church] and a fine example of this is the enrichment of the new high altar with motifs taken from the old". This latter emphasis fits in with the wish expressed by Bishop Moverley for his ordination, that it mixes old and new. His chosen motto *Nova et Vetera* echoes the same sentiment.

J.J. Frame had won the contract and work was undertaken that affected the sanctuary, the pulpit and, indirectly, the Baptistery. Paul Helliwell remembers well the scaffolding within the church because, besides the obvious changes to the major liturgical features, the whole interior was re-decorated, the heating and electrical systems upgraded and the floor renewed. Somehow, over several months, Sunday Mass continued. Teams of parishioners worked each Saturday to clear the dust created by the various building works. During these works Sheffield Cathedral welcomed St. Marie's to celebrate weekday Masses there. A commemorative plaque in the floor of the Anglican Cathedral was placed by the altar step, such was the goodwill generated at the time by this act of ecumenical fraternity.

The unveiling of the plaque in Sheffield Cathedral, showing the Bishop Gordon Fallowes of Sheffield, Bishop Gerald Moverley and Gerard Young

During the summer of 1972 on each weekday the Roman Catholic priests and people of St. Marie's celebrated Mass in this Cathedral Church while their own church in Norfolk Row was being restored.
This stone, unveiled in 1973 by the High Sheriff of Hallamshire on behalf of St. Marie's, records the gratitude to the Provost and Chapter for this act of Christian hospitality

The inscription on the plaque

130   The enthusiasm for the re-deployment of medieval arrangements in the Neo-Gothic revival, as at St. Marie's, led to the disregarding of changes to the physical layout of Catholic churches that followed the Council of Trent in the 16th Century, and included the discontinuance of screens and the separation of the congregation from the altar by an area for a choir.

The design proposals from J.J. Frame had been selected against competition.

Bartlett and Purnell Ltd. of Westminster made more than one proposal for the re-ordering of the sanctuary. In some senses they were least change options in that they retained the rood screen. In correspondence during August 1969 concerning their plans, the company made clear, *"It has been our endeavour, so far as possible, to revert to the church as it was originally conceived and not to move out any of the original work"*. On the other hand, they included a plan more radical than all others in that it brought the altar farthest forward and in front of the rood screen.

In this proposal the new altar would stand on a platform, under the central crossing of the church. This arrangement could make use of the transepts for congregation, adding to the number of people closer to the action at the altar. The altar would be raised on a sanctuary platform three steps up from the nave floor; with a further two steps to the altar. This would have been similar to the re-ordering in several major Gothic cathedrals in France (e.g. at Chartres or Notre Dame, Paris). The new altar itself would be stone and on 12 pillars for support, Gothic in style. A presider's chair would be on a platform near the rear of the sanctuary with a low wall behind it, all placed in front of the area occupied by the 1921 altar. This altar, complete with its alabaster panelled retable, would be moved to the Blessed Sacrament and replace the existing altar there.

A drawing to show the proposal to site a new altar in front of the rood screen

In another proposal involving the altar being placed in front of the rood screen, the 1921 altar would remain in place but the organ would be re-sited with the console in the upper Munster chapel with choir members singing from the St. Joseph's (Norfolk) Chapel. Both this proposal and yet another by T.C. Wilcocks Ltd., a local organ specialist, would necessitate a change in the organ's tracker mechanism from manual to electric, effecting the sound of the instrument. To accommodate the pipework in both proposals, an arched tunnel would be made through the re-sited organ mechanisms to the sacristy doorway. The organ pipes would be arranged above. The organist and console would be out of sight of the congregation but would have sight of the priest through the rood screen.

In the proposals involving the projected altar platform in front of the screen, there would be new reading places to either side.

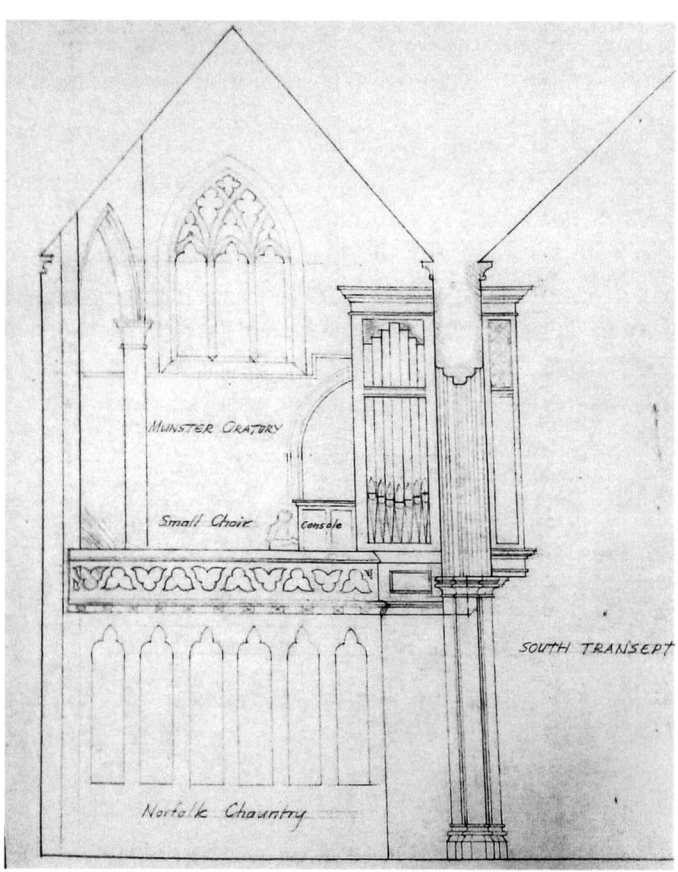

A drawing to show the proposal to move the organ and console to the Munster Chapel

The J.J. Frame proposal that was accepted removed the rood screen and, thereby, could retain a new altar within the existing sanctuary area whilst it being in full view of the nave, facilitating active participation by the congregation. The organ remained untouched, as did the 1921 High Altar. The choir stalls would go in what appears to have been a move towards more singing by the congregation perhaps without a formal choir. The altar steps would intrude much less in front of where the rood screen had been than in the other proposals. In all, this was a simpler design but with much greater impact in terms of opening up the whole liturgical space.

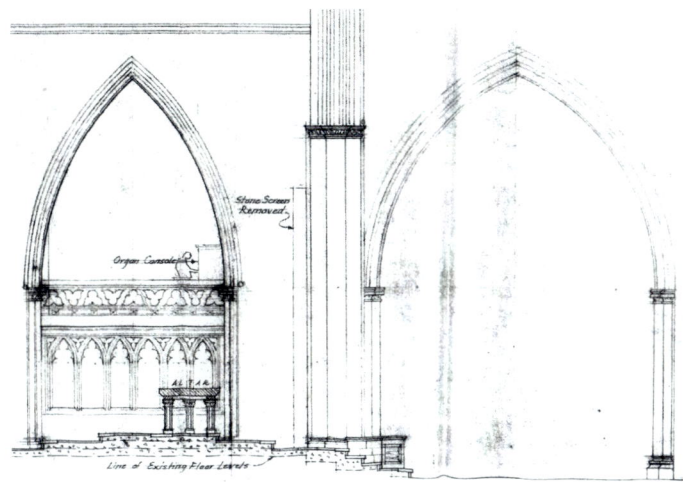

A proposal for the altar without a screen in the existing sanctuary area

The desire to make use of old features within the new was fulfilled in the decision to convert parts of the pulpit to serve as a three sided ambo for the reading of scriptures. Additionally, it was decided to convert other parts of the pulpit[131] into a baptismal font. This was to be placed on the sanctuary for baptisms to be more visible to the congregation whether celebrated within or outside the Mass[132].

The proposed design and siting of the baptismal font using parts of the former pulpit

The fine wooden pulpit at St. Marie's had been designed and carved by Arthur Hayball, a Sheffield craftsman. Completed by his daughter, Clara, after his death, it seems it was installed after 1889 since there is no mention of a pulpit in Charles Hadfield's description of St. Marie's published in 1889[133]. The complete pulpit and its canopy were highly decorated with symbolic imagery. Behind the preacher, instead of the more usual crucifix, there was a carved figure of the Good Shepherd. Two panels of the pulpit were carved as scenes. One depicted Christ preaching to disciples whilst the other showed St. Augustine preaching in 597 to the pagan king Ethelbert of Kent[134]. A range of carvings from the pulpit are now displayed in Cathedral House.

The pulpit before it was dismantled

In the parish newsletter for 27th August 1972, Mgr. Sullivan writes of the re-ordering work coming to an end. The Stations of the Cross had been reinstated, cleaned and 'modernized' by the removal of their heavy frames in order to focus on the figures. The new communion rails were in place, the metal uprights were those that had been removed 30 years earlier and had come back to St. Marie's from St. Theresa's with the help of a Mr. Lunt. All was ready for the celebration of Mass on the new High Altar.

131   The sounding board as a canopy and the pulpit base to contain the bowl of the font.
132   Later, parts of the choir stalls were re-used in a cathedra (bishop's chair) for Bishop Moverley as Bishop of Hallam.
133   *History of St. Marie's Mission and Church* pp 87-98.
134   As described by St. Bede in his *Ecclesiastical History of the English Church and People.*

The 1972 altar

On Friday 8ᵗʰ September 1972, the feast of the Birthday of Our Lady, Bishop Moverley consecrated the new High Altar, with Bishop Wheeler presiding as principal celebrant at the Mass. The relics from the 1921 altar were solemnly interred in the new altar surface. The re-ordering was complete.

By happy timing, within weeks of the completion of the interior work, work on cleaning the smoke blackened exterior of St Marie's began. The October 15ᵗʰ parish newsletter speaks of the work beginning and being paid for by "*the city fathers*" (i.e. Sheffield City Council) through funds made available by the Department of Environment for the improvement of the city.

The 1973 external cleaning as Norfolk Row is pedestrianised

135   Hadfield p.95.

Looking back from a time which gives significant attention to protecting heritage and to careful conservation, it is reasonable to ask why one of the proposals that preserved more artwork in St. Marie's was not chosen. But, at the time of the post Vatican II re-ordering there was, generally, far less concern for design dating from past times that prevented current needs being met. In addition, it is possible that bad feeling had developed between St. Marie's and Bartlett and Purnell Ltd. It was this company that had arranged the removal of seven medieval alabasters donated to St. Marie's before 1850 that were fixed to the wall beneath the altar in the Mortuary Chapel. The intention had been to sell these to raise money for the re-ordering. However, the alabasters were seriously damaged during the removal process, they then failed even to acheive the reserve price when auctioned at Sotherby's in London. Mgr. Sullivan, in a subsequent letter to the company writes, "*It seems to me a great pity that on your advice the Nottingham Alabasters were removed with the hope that sufficient money would be gained to pay for the alterations to the church, and instead I received a bill for £251. 12s 6d... In talking the matter over with Bishop Moverley, we have agreed that either he or I will call to bring the Alabasters back to Sheffield in the very near future.*

There were at the time (even before more recent years of heightened awareness of heritage and conservation) those who felt that the alterations to the interior of St Marie's in 1972 were excessive and destructive of the 1850 design. But the decisions made centred on the needs of the worshipping community in changed times and in accord with a Council of the Church.

A key aspect of the changes that drew criticism was the removal of the rood screen, a gift in 1850 from the Sheffield artist and prominent parishioner Henry Bulmer. It was carved by Arthur Hayball, whose studios and family home were in Cavendish Street, and then decorated in paints by Bulmer. Writing to a correspondent in 1990, Bishop Moverley was clear in his defence of the decision to remove the rood screen. It had revealed the "*glory of the East window, which nobody was able to see*". Interestingly, Hadfield, in his 1889 history of St. Marie's refers to the screen in 1850 being a "*much combated feature*"[135].

Separately, and concerning criticism of the removal of the mensa (altar table) from the 1921 altar, he replied, "*When they pulled down the first altar ...they encased the broken mensa etc, of the first altar beneath the mensa of the second altar. In our refurbishment of 1971/1972 a new altar was built towards the front of the sanctuary; and so the original effect should not be lost and at the same time there should not be two altar on the sanctuary, the second altar mensa was taken away and the [decorated* stone] *front of the altar was recessed into the reredos. The relics which had been in the first and the second now repose in the third one".*

On the criticism about the loss of the wooden pulpit, the bishop accepted that *"The original pulpit... was dismantled; but here again it was not destroyed or lost. It was used to make the existing lectern and a moveable baptismal font. The whole effect is extremely pleasant".* The moveable font, however, ceased to be used and was removed within 20 years as Baptisms returned to being conducted at the font in the original baptistery at the back of the church. The carved woodwork was discarded.

Towards a New Diocese

In the years between 1850 and 1880, Bishop Cornthwaite of Beverley had recognized that the diocese established in 1850 for the whole of Yorkshire had already become too large. Rapid and huge industrial expansion had taken place both in the North of the diocese, especially in Leeds, Bradford, Halifax and Huddersfield and, in the South, in Sheffield, Doncaster, Barnsley and all across the mining area between these centres. To respond to these changes, in 1878, two dioceses were formed - the Diocese of Middlesbrough to serve the civic areas of Yorkshire known as the North and East Ridings, and the Diocese of Leeds to serve the West Riding. Bishop Cornthwaite became the first Bishop of Leeds, whose diocese extended southwards to the Derbyshire border which then lay just south of Sheffield's centre.

Over the century between 1878 and the 1970s, both industrial manufacturing and coal mining had expanded and the total population living in Leeds Diocese had risen to above a million. In 1972 the Local Government Act had re-organized the civic boundaries of the three Yorkshire Ridings. In 1974 the Metropolitan Counties of South Yorkshire and West Yorkshire were formed but they did not cover the same area as the former West Riding. New civic boundaries elsewhere resulted in the Leeds Diocese having schools and churches within the new counties of North Yorkshire, Humberside, Cumbria, Greater Manchester as well as Lancashire. A rationalizing of the boundaries of the diocese was needed.

The Bishop of Leeds, Gordon Wheeler, had for many years hoped to form a new diocese to cover the southern part of his diocese, the area now known as the County of South Yorkshire. Such a move would both halve the population of the diocese and, just as importantly, acknowledge the distinction between the already very different characters of the northern and southern parts of the diocese. In the northern part, there was both a large rural area north of Leeds and a huge industrial belt including Leeds and Bradford, dominated by the wool and clothing industries. In the southern part of the diocese the predominant industries were coal-mining

The interior in 1973 showing the new altar, the cathedra and new ambo with the pews, new in 1957

Bishop Gordon Wheeler,
principal consecrator of Bishop Moverley

and steel manufacture. The two parts of the diocese had little in common and lacked any cohesion or common centres – Sheffield, for example, had no reason to look to Leeds for civic or any other facilities. It was these differences (and the huge size of the diocese) that caused Bishop Wheeler, in 1967, to appoint an auxiliary bishop to serve this southern area.

By 1966, the Second Vatican Council has decreed that, across the world, *"...a prudent revision of diocesan boundaries is to be undertaken as soon as possible"*[136]. The intention included that bishops be accessible and closer to their priests and people and be able to carry out pastoral visits to parishes across his diocese. Smaller dioceses were anticipated. The reckoning was that the maximum size for a diocese should be about 200,000 people and the minimum about 80,000.

That same year the Bishop's Conference of England and Wales set up a commission to study possible restructurings. The discussion paper resulting was delayed until 1974 because of the pending civic boundary changes. When published, it included the idea of splitting the Leeds Diocese between its north and south. During Lent of 1974, Bishop Wheeler visited each of the seven deaneries in the south of the Leeds diocese. Whilst some priests regretted the idea of becoming part of a diocese other than that into which they had been ordained, most were content. But reservations were expressed over the financial viability of so small a diocese and the lack of rural or non-industrial parishes.

By 1976 the Conference of Bishops for England and Wales had given formal approval to the proposal for a new diocese in South Yorkshire. A repeat series of visits to deaneries in 1977 found more enthusiasm among priests of the Leeds diocese who would be affected by the change because the plan now included more rural areas in the proposed diocese. For example, it was now planned to include the parishes in the new County of Humberside that were south of the river Humber (previously part of the Diocese of Nottingham). Further consultation resulted in a view that the rural district west of South Yorkshire, known as High Peak, should also be included in the new diocese.

Meanwhile, the Bishop of Nottingham had consulted with the clergy of the 9 parishes of South Humberside. A key finding was that these parishes wanted to remain as a single pastoral deanery, regardless of which diocese they were in. There were at the time three options open. These parishes could have been ceded to a redesigned Middlesbrough Diocese that would incorporate the whole county of Humberside, both sides of the Humber. They could have become part of the new diocese based on South Yorkshire and in need of more rural parishes. Or they could remain in Nottingham Diocese. But once the decision had been made not to include the south area of the Humber in a re-designed Middlesbrough Diocese, the debate was between the bishops of Leeds and Nottingham alone. And it seems that there was no enthusiasm on the part of Nottingham to give up parishes to a new diocese designed to ease the burden on Leeds. Nottingham would not, in any case, gain anything from the new diocese.

The Gatehouse of Padley Hall
which contains the chapel of the martyrs

Much debate seems to have followed, now centred now on the parishes of High Peak that would be a loss to Nottingham Diocese. These included the parishes of Buxton, Chapel-en-le Frith, Glossop, Hadfield, Marple Bridge and New Milton. But once it had been established that these towns looked towards Manchester or Derby

136   The Decree on the Bishop's Pastoral Office *"Christus Dominus"* para 22.

as local centres (and not towards Sheffield) they were excluded from the design of the new diocese. Only a few parishes outside South Yorkshire would be included in the new diocese and these, despite long debate, would include the parish of Hathersage. This would be a bitter loss to Nottingham Diocese because it contained the historic and much valued place of pilgrimage at Padley.

In February 1978 (only two years before the new diocese was created) the *Proposal for the Creation of a New Diocese in South Yorkshire, South Humberside and High Peak* was drawn up at the request of Bishop Wheeler of Leeds. This included the 10 parishes of Humberside, south of the Humber, and 8 parishes of High Peak additional to Bamford and Hathersage, which were accepted as naturally within the environs of Sheffield/ Chesterfield. However (and it seems after further debate) the 1978 Proposal stated: *"The ancient Chapel at Padley should remain within the Diocese of Nottingham because of its intimate connection with that diocese"*.

In the end, the Petition to Rome for the creation of the new diocese listed 50 parishes with 74 priests to be transferred from Leeds Diocese. From Nottingham Diocese the final totals for transferring were 11 parishes with 15 priests. The ancient chapel of Padley was, it was finally decided, to transfer to the new diocese as a location within its parish of Hathersage[137].

The area of the new diocese having (at last) been decided, there remained the question of the name for the diocese and the location of its cathedral church.

The area covered by the Diocese of Hallam

It had been the practice, since the 1850 restoration of Catholic hierarchy (bishoprics and parishes) in England and Wales that, as a courtesy, no Catholic diocese would take the name of an already existing Anglican diocese. Since, by the 1970s, both Sheffield and Doncaster had a bishop within the Church of England, the new diocese could not take on either of these names. Yet the name of a diocese should describe its location. Fortunately, in ancient

times there had been an identifiable region covering the environs of Sheffield and the Eastern Peak District. This was known as Hallam or Hallamshire. Additionally, an ancient name existed for the area south of the Humber that was intended to be included in the new diocese. This was known as The Vale of Axholme. Hence the 1978 Proposal records, *"a descriptive and distinct title of the new diocese would be "The Diocese of Axholme and Hallam"*. With the subsequent decision to leave the south Humberside parishes in Nottingham Diocese, the name proposed in the Petition to Rome for the creation of the new diocese became "The Diocese of Hallam".

The original drawing for the Coat of Arms for Bishop Moverley

Discussion about where the centre of the new episcopal see might be seems to have been brief. During the period when it was thought that the diocese might stretch from Grimsby in south Humberside across to the western side of the High Peak, the large and imposing new church of St Peter in Chains at Doncaster was built. Some say that this was mooted as a suitable centre for such a diocese. However, even in the 1978 Proposal for this larger diocese, it was recognized that more than one third of the population of the new diocese would live in Sheffield and that the local religious leaders, Anglican, Methodist and Free Churches, all centred themselves in Sheffield. The Proposal concludes, *"There would be loss of esteem for the Church were the episcopal see to be elsewhere"*.

Happily the Proposal recorded, *"There is, too, in the city of Sheffield, a magnificent church which is eminently suitable for a cathedral, namely the church of St. Marie… tastefully refurbished in recent years for the new liturgy it is spacious and imposing for episcopal ceremonies…"*.

137   To this day the annual diocesan pilgrimage to Padley is a joint event for the people and clergy of both the new diocese and Nottingham. It is frequently attended by both bishops.

Now at last and on a third occasion, the scale and grandeur of a building constructed, to my mind, as a potential cathedral, had achieved cathedral status. In 1850, despite its cathedral-like design and its construction during the discussions to form a diocese for Yorkshire, St. Marie's failed to be chosen as a cathedral. Instead; a church at Beverley became the cathedral of Yorkshire. Again in the 1880s, the extensive extensions to sacristies and a grand corridor for forming processions, undertaken during the time of discussion to form a second diocese in Yorkshire, St. Marie's failed to be chosen as a cathedral. Instead, a church in Leeds became the new cathedral. This time the longstanding features of St. Marie's, some tailor made

for a cathedral, and its adaptation for new liturgy, were recognized and St. Marie's was to be elevated to be a cathedral church.

On 30th May 1980 the Petition to the Holy Father was granted. Pope John Paul II had given permission to found the new Diocese of Hallam and its cathedral church was to be St. Marie's. All that was now needed was for the first Bishop of Hallam to be installed in his cathedral and for the clergy and parishes of the new diocese to welcome their new bishop. The date for this was set for the inauguration Mass and the installation of the Bishop. It was to be 3rd July 1980.

Bishop Moverley after his installation as Bishop of Hallam, 3rd July 1980

The cathedral church of St. Marie

Appendix One
The Memorial Altar Of 1921:
How much of the original Pugin altar is left?

The original High Altar of St. Marie's was described by Charles Hadfield[1] as having been designed by the great Victorian Gothic Revival architect and designer Augustus Welby Pugin. It was this altar that Canon Dolan replaced. But, at St. Marie's, the High Altar as now seen has long been referred to as by Pugin[2]. So how much remains of the altar that Pugin designed? A very unclear photograph in Hadfield's history[3] provides some information.

A sketch of the Pugin design for part of the altar at St. Marie's exists[4]. It shows only the central tabernacle and throne above. Something similar can be seen in a

photograph taken in 1889. But the canopy is clearly less tall than the Pugin sketch and without the proposed statues either side of the throne. Nevertheless the structure present in 1889 is described by Hadfield[5] as:

"...a structure of the most exquisite detail and workmanship. The door is enamelled metal, deep set amidst enriched mouldings and panelling, whilst on either side, delicate as if carved in ivory, instead of stone, are minute statuettes of angels "harping on their harps"; growing upwards, an open niche or throne, for the exposition of the Blessed Sacrament, is formed, crowned by an elegant canopy of pinnacles".

A photograph from 1889 or before, showing the original alter. The Pugin Reredos can be seen against the East wall

1   In his A History of St. Marie's Mission and Church (page 98) he writes *"The western window was carried out by Messrs. Hardman and Co., of Birmingham, and is, with the high altar and reredos, from designs by A.W.Pugin".*
2   Though it is known that Pugin's associate, Theodore Phiffers, built the original altar and the reredos on the East wall.
3   Opposite page 82.
4   This is reproduced in Patricia Spencer-Silver's book *George Myers: Pugin's Builder* page 93 (2010 Gracewing).
5   Hadfield p.91.

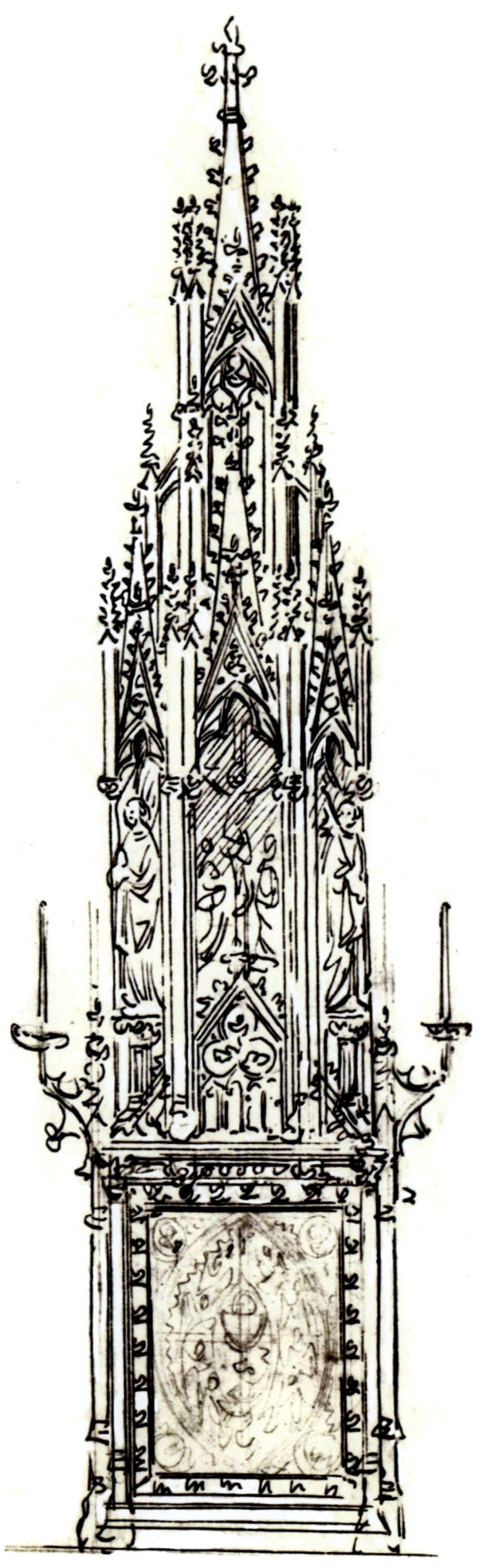

*Pugin's drawing for the proposed tabernacle
for St Maries Church, Sheffield
(courtesy of Myers Family Trust and Dr Timothy McCann)*

Clearly the canopy, not dissimilar to the Pugin design, was removed in 1921, but is the tabernacle of the 1921 altar part of the original Pugin inspired design? Whilst the proportions of the 1921 tabernacle are similar to those of the original altar, detail discernable from the 1889 photographs shows miniature buttresses at the tabernacle base and fine vertical carving to either side of the door. In addition, the top surface of the original tabernacle is flat, whereas in the 1921 altar it is gabled and with an integral and very simple throne. The decoration around the tabernacle doors and of the doors themselves is much simpler than what is visible of the earlier structure in photographs or described by Hadfield. It seems clear that the central structure possibly based on Pugin's design was removed in the 1920 rebuild.

*A close-up of the tabernacle canopy
as it appears in Hadfield's 1889 history*

A second debate has concerned whether the fine detail of the alabaster retable, rising from the altar surface, is a part of the original altar. Again the old photographs help. Despite the expectation that there would have been a retable on the original altar to match the 1850 reredos against the East wall behind the altar, there was nothing to either side of the tabernacle described by Hadfield nor visible in the early photograph. The photograph shows the plain area of the East wall reredos visible behind the altar.

The plain design of this reredos on all parts of it that could have been hidden by a retable contrasts with the fine ornamentation at the sides that would have been visible even with a retable on the original altar. This suggests that a retable may have been planned to the height of the tabernacle, thus hiding the plain areas of the reredos behind. But this was never built, probably because of lack of funds. Hadfield notes the overall financial burden that had been incurred by the time the church was opened in 1850.

In 1921, at the time of the consecration of the new altar, Sheffield's main newspaper[6] makes no reference to re-used material from the Pugin altar. Instead it praises the design of the new:

"The design presented formidable difficulties enough, but the work was readily undertaken by Messrs Hardman and Pippet of Birmingham, and right well have they carried out their task. Made of stone, richly painted and decorated, the new altar stands out as a very striking feature in the sanctuary of St. Marie's. The idea adopted by the artist in designing this work has been based on the colour schemes of the illuminations painted by monks in the fifteenth century in England and France. In the reredos are four recesses, over-hung by delicate tabernacle work, in which are alabaster bas reliefs very exquisitely carved and decorated with colour and gold".

One of the four alabaster carvings in the retable

One of the squares with carving resembling a military medal

Looking now at the 1921 design, there appear to be two different styles intermingled. On the one hand there are squares at the base with strong carvings resembling military medals. On the other hand, there is the delicacy of the carved angels between these medallions. Similarly, there is symmetry between the carved niches for the four lower angels and the decoration of the upper part of the reredos. The four alabaster square panels built into the 1921 retable are extremely delicately carved with fine neo-gothic artistry. Both the delicate supporting angels between the medallions beneath the altar table and the alabaster scenes are, it seems to me, on a par with the delicacy of the Pugin design of the East wall reredos[7].

The new 1921 tabernacle

6   *Sheffield Daily Telegraph* June 22nd 1921.
7   The commission to build the 1921 altar was awarded to Hardman and Howell, a firm continuing Pugin principles. Elphage and Oswald Pippett were almost certainly involved in the design hence the degree of Puginesque work.

The apparent difference in delicacy and style in different parts of the altarpiece may reflect only the differences between direct copies of medieval illustrations for some detail and new elements of the design. The plain tabernacle, throne and the military-looking medallion carvings beneath the altar surface seem in contrast to the more medieval looking elements.

It is not clear what the *"formidable difficulties"* in arriving at the final design might have been. It is possible that these were about differing tastes and design ideas. But it seems clear that the whole structure was designed afresh, without any Pugin work being included.

In 2012, during the re-ordering of the cathedral, it became necessary to de-construct one side of the 1921 retable to its base in order to strengthen the structure. In removing stones at one side, carved surfaces and painted patterns were discovered on the inside of these[8]. It seems likely that some stones from the original Pugin altar had been re-used in part of the 1921 altar. The stone area beneath the original altar surface is not visible in any early photographs because of a cloth frontal hanging from the front edge of the altar. The re-use of stones from that original altar would have been a cost saving and could add weight to the supposition that other (and carved) parts of the Pugin altar might also have been re-used in 1921.

Whatever the complete truth regarding the age of the various elements of the altar as now seen, the Memorial Altar is, without doubt, one of the key artistic features of St. Marie's but one whose provenance may never be fully known.

What is clear, however, is that the 1850 reredos along the East wall designed by Pugin with rich angel decoration to either side survived in 1921 because of the choice of the current design. Indeed the 1921 altar economically makes use of the Pugin reredos to extend the decoration of the altar to either side. Alternative designs were made and rejected, including a much larger and more completely neo-Gothic design which would have blocked from view (or required the destruction of) one of the few Pugin elements of St. Marie's. The smaller scale of the 1921 altar ensures that pre-existing decoration associated with the original altar is visible and extends the decoration across the full width of the East sanctuary wall.

A section of the reredos designed by Pugin against the East wall

8   The colours and patterns discovered were then replicated in the painted pattern in the sides of the altarpiece.

Appendix Two
John Maher
Parishioner and Survivor of a Japanese Prisoner of War Camp

*John Maher aged 20
before embarkation to Singapore*

The following is taken from a testimony given by Eileen Maher, a longstanding parishioner and widow of John Maher[1].

In the early days of World War II, John Maher became a prisoner of the Japanese and endured the prison camps, harsh discipline and gruelling work building the infamous Burma railway and the bridge over the river Kwai built by British and allied prisoners of war.

Eileen Maher recalls

"Each year on Remembrance Sunday until his death in 2006, at the end of the 10.30 Requiem Mass, John used to stand at the top of the sanctuary steps eyes front, firmly to attention, wearing his medals. There he would recite clearly and strongly the famous lines of the poem - 'They shall grow not old as we who are left grow old...'

He would then proudly carry the wreath of poppies to the war memorial at the back of church where it was blessed and laid.[2]

"Unlike so many others, John did grow old. He was 87 when he died, but many of his Army colleagues perished in the infamous POW camps in Thailand or in building the Railway of Death and the Bridge over the river Kwai.

"He was 20 when he was called up into the Army, and after a stint in Sunderland and fire watching on the docks in Liverpool, was sent on a troopship to the Far East. His ship was bombed and caught fire outside Singapore. He had no option but to jump overboard into Singapore harbour offering a prayer as he did so. He was later rescued after clinging to debris for some time and so became a prisoner of war of the Japanese.

"John spent four years of his life in captivity in appalling conditions, living in palm covered huts with a diet of rice and little else. The Japanese were known for their cruelty and rigid discipline. Conditions were very harsh. However, the Catholic men were lucky in that they had a Catholic priest, a Fr Cowan, with them in the camp. By 'borrowing' bits of wood and various materials they were able to fashion a Catholic chapel and they used it regularly for Mass. One day they realised they were running short of altar bread, and would be unable to celebrate Mass any more. Some time later a Japanese officer came to the camp and asked for the Catholic priest. Everyone 'froze', even in humid jungle temperatures. Fr Cowan and the officer went inside the little church... appearing some time later smiling and looking relaxed. The officer, it turned out, was a Catholic and hearing about the shortage of altar bread had brought some! It was a dangerous thing for him to do and had he been caught doing it, the penalties would have been severe.

"His Catholic faith played a great part in John's survival. He believed in God and put his trust in Him. Many others gave up and died. Many men died from cholera which was rampant in such conditions, where there was no clean water, nor proper sanitation and very little medication. John was a cholera carrier but never actually had it. When he went to war he was a 6 feet tall, healthy young man. When he came home 4 years later, he weighed just 6 stone and looked like a living skeleton.

1   John was first invited to do this by Monsignor Sullivan in the early 1970s.

*Fr. Cowan with the senior Japanese Officer
in the prison camp*

John by the memorial stone at the church in Wymondham

"Fr. Cowan, always said that if he survived to go home he would set up a shrine to the men who suffered so much during their captivity. He did survive, thank God, and the National Shrine to the Far East Prisoners of War is now in the Catholic church at Wymondham in Norfolk. The church contains a Book of Remembrance of all the men who died. It was hand-written on vellum by one of John's Catholic friends from Sunderland, and is a testimony to all the brave men who fought and died in the Far East during the Second World War. They were only released after the atomic bomb was dropped on Nagasaki otherwise, John said, the Japanese would never have surrendered.

"In later, happier times and after marrying and having 4 children, John used to help students from the University who were researching the war, and who would come and interview him. He is mentioned in several theses. He also befriended several Japanese students who came to St. Marie's while studying in Sheffield. He had no bitterness

in him, and talked readily about his experiences, both to journalists and on the radio, always mentioning his Catholic Faith. John was a very forgiving man and always said that there was good and bad in all nationalities.

"Each year in August, until 60 years after the end of the 2nd World War, John arranged an inter-denominational Service of Remembrance held in Barkers Pool at the War Memorial. Various ministers and, sometimes, the parish priest from St. Marie's led the service. Prayers were said. Wreaths of white flowers were laid. Tears were shed. The bugler played the Last Post and a proud, and often tearful survivor would declare...

*'They shall grow not old, as we who are left grow old.
Age shall not weary them nor the years condemn.
At the going down of the sun and in the morning,
we will remember them!'
Amen.
Rest in Peace."*

After the war against Japan had ended in 1946, John was freed from captivity and returned to Sheffield and to civilian life. He developed skill and qualification in woodworking and carpentry, joining the council's Works Department. In 1963 he married Eileen Loomes and, with a growing family moved home, closer to St Marie's.

John soon became a stalwart helper, especially with unassuming tasks at the back of church. Over time John became, for almost 40 years, a reliable welcoming presence each Sunday. Regularly serving as sidemen and at the Offertory collections, John became a natural leader of this group. At the larger and more crowded services during each year, John would organise the helpers at the back of church, especially in assisting the smooth flow of the congregation, for example, to Holy Communion, He aimed always for quiet reverence and avoiding disorder.

As a qualified and skilful carpenter, John designed and built a wooden platform that rested on the sanctuary steps and was used when needed, to extend the sanctuary area forward by several feet. It was first used for the pageant presented as part of the 1989 centenary celebrations of the consecration of St. Marie's.

John died in June 2006 and was buried at City Road Cemetery. John is remembered as a much loved, sociable and respected member of the parish community.

John Maher at a Far East memorial service in the 1970s

Mgr. Sullivan leads the Far East Prisoner of War Association memorial service on the Sunday nearest Victory over Japan Day

Appendix Three
A Transcript of the interview with Cecil Higgins
– the man who saved the stained glass of St. Marie's

Cecil Higgins, some years before 1939

"This is Mr Cecil Higgins and I am invited here this afternoon to explain what happened to the stained glass et cetera in the cathedral church here of St. Marie's. That was before it was a cathedral. The incumbent then was a gentleman by the name of Canon Bradley, who I had to report to.

"When, of course, the Second World War came, it was a matter of considering what to do with all the stained glass in the city because of the fact that they expected Sheffield to be a prime target for bombing, which certainly it turned out to be. And so, consequently, first of all I was requested by the Provost of Sheffield, the Reverend A.C.E. Jarvis at the cathedral, to start there and then to go through all the Sheffield Diocese to remove all stained glass which was removable at the time, and those which weren't removable were to be boarded up outside and inside and, in between the boarding and the

actual stained glass window we poured in sand to form a cushion so that when there was the blast and vibrations, it wouldn't break the glass. And that was done only for those windows that were considered to be too fragile to attempt removal of them. Because after, say, about 100 years (and most of the glass in the cathedral [St. Marie's] was round about that time), the lead canes which held the glass together are perishable and you can almost peel it off like tape, and so since the weight of the window is supported by saddle bars at about 18 inch intervals and let into the stone work at either side. And the window then is tied with copper ties to the [saddle] bar. But, of course, for removal you have to remove the bars first, untie them and remove the saddle bars. And, consequently, when of course the lead has got to that perishable state, it means that if you untie it from the bars, the weight of the glass bulges the window and the lead, of course, just can't hold it. These we boarded up inside and outside and poured sand in.

"And we had to go through the whole of the Sheffield Diocese which goes out as far as Goole in East Yorkshire. And, anyways, whilst we were doing that, of course, we conveniently (for our convenience) decided to look also at any Roman Catholic churches who had requested that their glass should be removed as well. And this [St. Marie's] was one, of course, and this was the first one, naturally, being next door to the [Anglican] cathedral. We weren't going to take scaffolding and everything to another part of the diocese and then come back here. So we moved here. And then from here we went to Rotherham Parish Church and we went to St. Bede's at Masbrough in Rotherham. And we worked it like that.

"When we got here [to St. Marie's] though, the priest was, as I say, Canon Bradley. He was the priest in charge. He called me in to the presbytery here and said, 'Now then', he said, 'I want you to look at our windows and decide which should be removed and which should stay in situ to be boarded up'. And so, consequently, I was dispatched to come down here. I was only in my mid-twenties then, but the firm that I worked for was Robertson and Russell Ltd with studios at 43 Carver Street next to St. Matthew's Church. They were manufacturers of stained glass. I'd gone there from Sheffield School of Art in 1926 as an apprenticed designer and painter of church stained glass windows. And, consequently, as I say, war came.

"I remember the outbreak of war on the Friday and hearing all the newsboys running up Division Street shouting 'War, it's war!', 'Germany has invaded Poland!' And I can remember the financial director of the company (there were three directors of Robertson and Russell Ltd). There were 20 – 40 of us employed there. We were the biggest, actually, in the South Yorkshire area. Straight away the financial director said to me, 'Well, it looks as though we shall be losing you if you are medically fit enough to go into the services'. And so, of course, when my age group came up to register, I had to register. I particularly wanted the navy. I registered for the navy. I even volunteered for submarine service – to my wife's horror and disgust. When I'd had my medical, they asked me 'What service would you prefer? Navy, Army or Air Force?' I said 'Navy'. But he said, 'I'm sorry. You'll have no chance of getting into the Navy with your call-up [group] because all your call-up has to go into army regiments to make them up to strength after the losses at Dunkirk'. And so, straight away, I was assigned to the army and sent to Selby, there to be trained with the West Yorks Regiment.

"Straightaway, of course, the firm said (1939, this was), 'Well, we've got to get all the glass out before you're called up. We've only got 12 months before you're likely to be called up for the Army. So we want you to get all this glass removed by then'.

"And my immediate boss at the company was a professional artist who exhibited at the Royal Academy and Paris Salon and places like that. His name was George Hammond Steel. He was a Sheffield man. He said, 'Look. You're more used to churches than I am'. Because he didn't profess to being a believer at all really. And so he says, 'I'm going to put you in charge of removing all this glass'. And so I was given the responsibility.

"So, first of all, I thought, 'Well, we have to go down to the cathedral to start there first. Then we've got to take it as we can arrange it for our convenience to cover it as quickly as possible'. There was a dozen fellows working with me at all time. What I did was that I went to each particular church that we were going to remove work from and I examined every window and marked them up, this one to stay in situ and be boarded up… I assessed whether they were safe to be removed or whether they were all right to be removed and put into crates to be kept for the duration of the war. I would go to each particular church and they [the clergy] would tell me if any windows were of particular interest to them…

"And so with that I eventually, after the cathedral, came here [to St. Marie's]. Canon Bradley took me into the church and showed me all the windows and that, and he said that they were particularly keen to save the East Window and the Baptistery window – I remember that

with St. Oswald king and martyr and one or two others he pointed out. I can't clearly remember now, because, after all, it's half a century ago. I've been round all the churches and seen that much stuff. Anyway, he wanted those removing. Oh, and he wanted the West window removing.

"And so I made sketches of every window, just rough sketches, with subject matter on and any inscriptions, you know, memorials or even Latin inscriptions, for the purpose of being able to identify them and their position and returning them afterwards. And every drawing that I did it as marked, say, 'East window to chancel' or 'West window'. And so I then had those drawing printed in triplicate one set was left with the clergy at the church from which it had been removed, the second one was left in the files of the company in Carver Street, the third set was put into a cylindrical, watertight container and put into the crate with the actual window. And then the crates were stenciled like 'St. Marie's Canon Dolan window' or 'East Window to chancel, St. Marie's' and so on. Because I was thinking, 'Well, I don't know how long the war's going to go on for. I didn't even know whether I'd be the one responsible for putting them back'. But, in the mercy of God, I was. And so, straightway I thought, 'This will help considerably to know where they came from, what position in the church and what the subject matter was'.

"And the next things that puzzled me - and I said this to the directors of the company - I said, 'It's all right removing all this stuff, but where are we going to put it all'. I knew we had about three floors high in Carver Street Company but, even then, it was in a central position and was likely to get blitzed. They [the windows] were in as much danger as if they'd been left in the church.

Nunnery Colliery in 1940

"And so I got in touch with the Nunnery Colliery at Handsworth. And they said, 'Well look, we'll let you use a disused working of the colliery to store them in for the duration of the war, but they'd be stored at the owners' own risk. We're not having the responsibility'. So I says, 'That's good enough for the time being. We haven't any time to argue'.

"So as they were taken out, they were transported to the Nunnery Colliery at Handsworth. I went down [at the time when the first windows were to be stored in the mine] with two miners on bogies and saw where they were going to be stacked, at the side of the track, standing up on end – the safest position for them. And as we were going down, with the light on my helmet, I could see waves so I said, 'Hey just a minute. Is that water down there?' And so one of the miners said, 'It's water all right, up to the roof there'. I said, 'Why? Don't you work this?'. He says, 'No we don't. The working there is flooded'. He says, 'But there's a pump for this water and it's our job (pointing to his mate) to keep that pump working to keep the level down to where you see it now. And it's pumped off for the coke ovens at Handsworth'. So he said, 'You'll be alright where we're going to stop. You'll be well clear of that level and you can stack the windows at the side of the track, both sides'. Which I agreed to, and we did that.

"But one thing I will always remember with regard to this place, St. Marie's, was when we came to put them back after the war (I went into the Army in 1940 and came out in 1946). The first thing when the firm knew I'd been demobbed, they said to me, 'You'd better come down. Everybody's panicking to get their windows out'. And so, anyway, I went down to the firm and they said, 'When you've done the cathedral, St. Marie's want theirs putting back'. Well, in the natural order of things we should come here anyroad; it was most convenient for us.

"I was looking around, but the tragedy of it was – and this is the absolute gospel truth - you might not believe it – but during the war, and it must have been very early on, the pump broke down in that water. And because it was at owners' risk, the colliery never bothered to get it restored, with the result that the water came right up the working and submerged the crates and everything. Well it [the water] doesn't affect stained glass, of course; oh no, they could be under water for years and years, but the lead it did. And also the crates which were made of inch thick timbers, soaked in creosote. You've got to remember, we hadn't had any time to mess about. You'd got to get on with it and get it done. And so there was a certain amount of risk taken, which was certainly better than leaving them where they were for the Sheffield Blitz that came afterwards – very soon.

"And so, after the war, do you know, when I came back and started to get the stuff out of the Nunnery Colliery, we didn't get even one watertight container. We never found one! Where they went to we didn't know. The planks of the crates had all rotted and the glass had just dropped down into the grey mud…twelve inches…And so the only other chance was to get the set of copies that the clergy had got.

"And so I came here. I came in the door I've come in today and I was shown into Canon Bradley's room and he was sat back in a low chair. There were newspapers all around him – he'd let them drop to the floor. So I said, 'Good afternoon'. So he looked at me. 'Should I know you?' he said. 'How did you get in here?' I said, 'I've come through the front door'. And so, believe it or not, he looked at me as if he'd never seen me in his life before. So I said, 'Well, I've come about your stained glass'. So he stood up, straightened himself, knocked some cigarette ash off the front of him and then he says, 'Ah. Are you going to do it then?' I says, 'Yes, I'm going to put it back. You do want it put back?' He says, 'Of course I do. That's why I phoned up'. So I said, 'Well, I've come to see if you've got your copy of all the windows that were taken out that I gave to you'. 'Oh' he says, 'There's been six years of war. Didn't you know about that?' I said, 'I know about it all right. I've been in the army. But' I said, 'I want those now, because they've all been lost in the colliery. There's none there.' So he says, 'Well, I haven't got any'. I looked at him and said, 'You what?' He says, 'I haven't any. If you took 'em out, it's your responsibility. You see that they're put back. If you know you job, that's your job'. So I thought, 'Well, That's it.'

"Well, I always remembered that the centre light of the East Window, if I remember rightly, is a full length image of the Virgin and then there were little roundels in the others, either side, starting at the top left has, as I remember, scenes from the life of the Virgin, all through right to her death or Assumption in the bottom right hand corner. I remembered that the background glasses were red/blue, red/blue, like that. And, do you know, I spent *six weeks* just *sorting* that window out because it was all in bits like a jigsaw puzzle….Most of the pieces[of glass] were intact, but some were never found. So there might be one or two places where we've got ordinary glass in because we were told not to bother repainting things, just to get them put back up.

"Anyway, when I'd figured this East window out, which is a memorial to Hadfield, Calkwell and Davidson who were the architects, I got all the tracery pieces in place, of which there was a considerable amount, really. Anyway, I managed to sort these out. And one thing you should remember is that the painted side of the glass is always to the *inside* of the church. And so that simplified a lot that could have faced either way. And so we got them all back… wedging in with lead braces, so I could ask Canon Bradley to ascertain and assure me that they're all in the right positions – the tracery pieces and all the rest of it – [to check] that the window was correct before we seal it in permanently. So that was another case of Canon Bradley to come out of this building into the church.

"I asked Canon Bradley to come through to the church to confirm that I'd got the windows back correctly before sealing it with lead. I said, 'Because we haven't any drawings'. In the meantime, of course, in the early days of the war, 1940, the firm was burnt to the ground in Carver Street. We'd lost *everything*. So we'd lost everything in the colliery; we'd lost everything at the firm, and so we were entirely dependent on the clergy of the churches and their copy.

"Anyway, he came into the church with me and we stood at the West end and he got out a pair of opera glasses and has a look all over the East window. Then he said, 'Aye, you've done a good job.' I says, 'It's all right, is it?' 'All but the two pieces of tracery right in the apex'. He said, 'They should be the other way round'. I says, 'They shouldn't' He says, 'I'm telling you they should!' I says, 'How do you know they should? Can you remember all that?' He says, 'I can remember *that*. I know that one side of the tracery is all female saints and the other side is all male saints, and those two pieces in the apex contravene that order'. I says, 'They don't'. So he looked at me and says, 'Are you telling me they don't? I know they do.' I says, 'Well I know they don't'. He says, 'And how can *you* be so sure?'. I says, 'Well, if I turn them round, I'll put the paint on the *outside* and it shouldn't be outside'. I says, 'That's the reason I'm arguing they are in the right position'. So he says, 'Well, They should be the other way round'. I says, 'I'd be interested to know how you can be so sure. In the first place, can you remember all those details about this window?' Then he felt inside his cassock and brought out a book. It would be about that size and the frontispiece inside, when you opened it, was a full page colour reproduction of that window as it was when it was dedicated. I says to him, 'Have you had that all the time?' 'Yes I have'. I says, 'Do you realise…. Well, you're a dark horse, aren't you'? I says, 'Why didn't you tell me? I've had to do all that from memory. He says, 'Well I wanted to see how well you knew your job'. I says, 'Well I'll tell you how well I know my job - it's going to cost you another £600 that!' I says, 'I've spent *six weeks* sorting it out. That's why I know very well those two pieces of tracery are in the right place. If they're in the wrong place, it's because they've been painted wrong'. So he shows me this illustration. I says, 'Aye, they obviously have been painted wrong. They *do* want turning round'. So I says, 'We can easily turn these around'.

"And so he says, 'So you've spent six weeks sorting this out?' I say, 'Yes I have. There was no other way for it'. Then I says, 'If you'd have lent me that book we'd have been in the clear straight away'. So he says, 'Come round to the presbytery, I'll write you a cheque straight away'. So I did and we shook hands and that was it'…"

[Later in the interview, referring to work that Cecil has done on the outside of St. Marie's he continued…]

"'Somewhere in here there's a mounted and framed drawing of the gable cross at the East end [of St. Marie's]. That [drawing] was done by my boss, George Hammond Steel. But I had to get the details and measurements and make a sketch first. And so I got Dan O'Neil in Solly Street, who was a buildings contractor and who was Roman Catholic,and when Canon Bradley said, 'I want a detailed drawing of the cross up there', I said, 'That's no problem, but it will have to have a tower of scaffolding put up to it with a back rail, because I shall have to have a drawing board and I'll have to loll back and I shall have to measure the thing and draw it'. And then a proper drawing can be done to scale from my measurements'. He [Canon Bradley] says, 'Well, I want that drawing done, a precise one, because it is a very special cross on that gable. It's likely to get damaged if there's any bombing around here and we want to be able to reproduce it'. So I says, 'That's no trouble'.

The drawing of the gable cross by George Hammond Steel from a sketch by Cecil Higgins

"So Dan O'Neil put the scaffolding up, fastened it to the wall at intervals, and a little platform for me to stand on with a back rail. Well, I climbed up and got onto this little platform. I'd got a small board with paper on. I'd got my knee up against the wall. I leaned forward to get hold of this thing [the cross] but when I got hold of it, it started to come towards me. The thing had had a copper dowel through it [as a lightning conductor] and down

75

into the stonework of the East gable. And that copper dowel had corroded through, and so it was standing there by its own weight. So I pushed the thing back and came down quick I'll tell you! [laughs]. So I went into Canon Bradley and says, 'Hey, that thing is standing up there under its own weight – I nearly pulled it down'. So he says, 'You never have!' I say, 'I have! And I'm not going up there anyways to take any more measurements until Dan O'Neil has been up there and had a look at that'. So he [Canon Bradley] rang him up from here [in the presbytery]. Dan O'Neil was down in quick time…'You mean to tell me it is standing by its own weight?'. 'Yes' I says, 'It is. I nearly pulled the thing over'. So he says, 'I can't believe that'. So he went up and had a look. And he says, 'My word! You're right. The copper dowel has corroded. It's not holding it'."

[Later, when referring to the restoration of the West window, Cecil continued…]

"'When we put the West window back in situ, two top pieces of tracery there were missing. We never found those. Mind you, when you come to think about it, they'd disintegrated into the mud in the colliery'

"When I came back from the army, I rang the manager up at Handsworth colliery and said, 'We shall be coming down with a lorry to pick up some of the glass. Will there be some of your fellows there to take me down to help bring the crates up?' So he says, 'Don't worry about that Mr Higgins, we'll get them up for you'. Well, straightaway I was a bit suspicious. I thought, 'Oh. Why?' And when we got there, they'd got them up alright! But they'd got boxes about as square as the top of this table [a little less than a metre] and about that deep [same in depth]. And they'd gone down with shovels, these two miners, and they'd shovelled the mud up and all the glass with it and what was left of the crates and what was left of the lead work and everything like that and put it into these boxes indiscriminately! That's the absolute truth! It couldn't have been worse!

"So they were all at the top of the pit top when I got there. I thought, 'Oh dear. What have I come back to?' I said, 'Haven't you found any watertight containers?' 'What are they?' They asked. I said, 'There were some watertight containers, cylinders, with screw tops on, with drawings in each crate stating where it had come from, what positions in the church and what the whole matter [subject] was'".

[At this point in the interview, we were joined by Ted Cummings, a former parishioner who had heard that the interview was taking place and had come to offer his memories. After this brief interruption, Cecil resumed by talking about the reconstruction of the West window and how only two small pieces of glass from minor decoration near the top had been lost. Cecil continued…]

"… 'Those are the two'.

"With these pieces of tracery for the West window, we never found them. They must be somewhere in the mud of the colliery even now ….

"And so he [Canon Bradley] says, 'What can we do about that?' I say, 'Do you know who put that window in in the first place?' So he says, 'I think it was a Birmingham firm'. I says, 'Well I know of John Hardman studios in Newhall Hill, Birmingham, they do stained glass. It might have been them, Hardman's.' 'That's it' [said Canon Bradley]. 'I'm pretty sure I remember that name'. So he got in touch with them and they supplied two more pieces of tracery for that window"[1]."

[There are tiny clear pieces at top of West window where the pieces were lost in the mud - small areas in the decorated edges of top tracery are plain whereas the rest are gold/orange].

[The new visitor who joined us shortly before this point, clearly itching to join in with his memories. He interjected…]

"There was a chap called Jimmy Doyle, a coal merchant. He used to be the doorman [at St. Marie's]. In those days you paid a contribution of money[2]. Heenan [Bishop John Carmel Heenan as Bishop of Leeds from 1951 to 1957] knocked that on the head when he took over. He [Jimmy Doyle] used to sit at the door at the 11 o'clock Mass and he had contacts where you could get paint and things like that when you couldn't get any[3]. So we kept the place going. And around then he [Canon Bradley] wanted to have the windows put back in time for the 1950 celebrations [of the centenary of St. Marie's]. So that was 1947. Then Canon Bradley said 'The only way we're going to get the money – he wanted £1,000 – was through [door to door] collections. And the truth was that there was that many collections during the war for different things – one coming in, two during and maybe one coming out [of Mass]. It's quite true, that. Anyways, he decided and there were only two of us turned up

---

1   It is not clear what happened to these new pieces, if Mr Higgins' recollection is correct. It may well be that they arrived after the window was re-instated and never replaced the clear glass put in by Mr Higgins.

2   This seems to be the practice of paying to reserve a pew, usually with your name displayed with a card in a brass holder fixed to the pew. Those able to afford this could choose where sit. At St. Marie's, there were two seats reserved for the Duke and Duchess of Norfolk which they used whenever visiting Sheffield.

3   Due to rationing or general shortages of goods for sale.

Cecil Higgins celebrating his 100th birthday in 2012

[to volunteer] – Jimmy Doyle and myself. And we did the whole thing between us, collecting on four Sundays. I was to do Lodge Moor all the way down – all the posh houses who only wanted to give tuppence, but tuppence was a lot of money then. You were fortunate if you got a six penny piece – the old tanner. Anyway, he wanted £1,000[4] to get the stained glass back up out of the Nunnery pit, the Duke of Norfolk's. And we got £2,000. And I don't know what happened to the other £1,000, but I'm sure Canon Bradley could make good use of it. He was a great man. He didn't talk to everybody, but nevertheless, when you got to know him, he was brilliant."

Cecil Higgins was, by now, tiring and the interview didn't take off again from this point. Perhaps, too, Mr Higgins felt a bit overshadowed by the newcomer who didn't introduce himself and was as ebullient as he was.

Cecil Higgin's memories, gathered in 2003, provide not only the major insights reproduced here, but also unique information into the saving of the stained glass from the 18th Century chapel at Revill Grange, Stannington, given in Part One of this history.

Cecil Higgins remained faithful to his Methodist upbringing as is clear in the online interview with him conducted by Sheffield Star at his 100th birthday in 2012. In this interview, his generosity and convivial nature are evident and heartwarming.

---

4   It is not clear whether or not this sum included the additional charge of £600 for the six weeks of extra labour caused by the canon's withholding relevant information.

Bibliography

Anderson, Neil	*Forgotten Memories from a Forgotten Blitz* (Sheffield, ACM Retro, 2010)
Anderson, Neil	*Defiant! Sheffield Blitz 75th* (Sheffield, ACM Retro, 2010)
Evinson, Denis,	*The Lord's House: A History of Sheffield's Roman Catholic Buildings 1570 – 1991* (Sheffield Academic Press, 1991)
Fit, Michal (ed)	*Sixty Five Years of Polish Education in Sheffield 1950-2015* (privately published, 2015)
Hadfield, Charles	*A History of S. Marie's Mission and Church* (Sheffield: Pawson and Brailsford, Printers, 1889)
Hagerty, James	*William Gordon Wheeler – A Journey into the Fullness of Faith* (Leominster, Gracewing, 2015)
Hallam, Vic	*Silent Valley – Life in the Derwent Valley 1939-1945* (Sheffield, Sheaf Publishing Ltd, 1990)
Hemphill, A.	A *Guide to St. Marie's* (unpublished, 1973)
Hird, Nicholas	*Our Fathers of Faith – A biographical sketch of the men who served as Priests within the Diocese of Leeds* (unpublished, 2008)
Kucewicz, Anna	*The Immigrant Experience: The Reception of Polish Refugees and their Adaptation in Sheffield post 1945* (unpublished)
Sullivan, S.P.	*A Short History of St. Marie's* published with *St. Marie's History and Guide* (Leominster: Fowler Wright Books, 1988)
Unattributed	*The Centenary of the Convent of Notre Dame, Sheffield* (Exeter: Catholic Records Press, 1955)
Unattributed	*Sheffield Catholic Monthly* (of 1935, 1936, 1937, 1938, 1946. 1097, 1950 , 1951, 1952)
Walsh, Frank	*A History of St Theresa's* (unpublished)